stonian History Museum Right **Entrance, Balthasar restaurant**

Left **Orthodox Cathedral of Alexander Nevsky** Right **Swan Lake, Kadriorg Park**

Key to abbreviations
Adm *admission*

TALLINN'S TOP 10

TALLINN'S TOP 10

TOP 10 Tallinn's Highlights

Tallinn is one of northern Europe's historical gems, with a well-preserved Old Town encircled by surviving City Walls. Gothic houses and slender spired churches add unique character to its narrow streets. However, there is much more to Tallinn than the Old Town and it is well worth branching out to destinations such as Kadriorg Park to the east and the Estonian Open-Air Museum further west for a refreshing mix of woodland beauty and rural culture.

1 Town Hall Square

Swarming with locals and visitors both day and night, Town Hall Square is the focal point of Tallinn's Old Town. Looming above the square is one of the city's defining monuments, the starkly beautiful Town Hall *(see pp8–9)*.

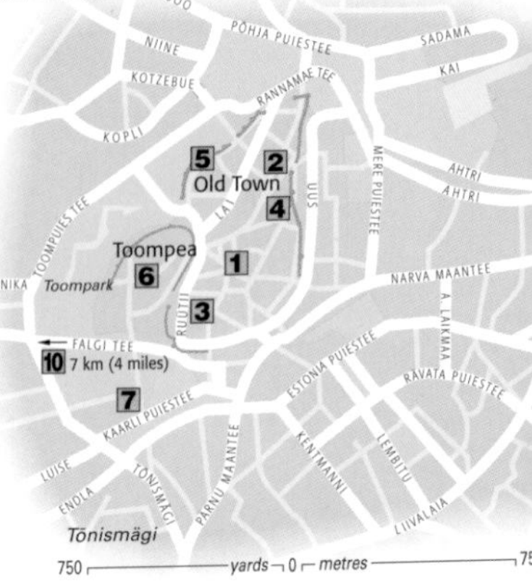

2 Pikk Street

There are few better ways of getting to grips with Tallinn's history than taking a stroll along Pikk Street, a cobbled alleyway lined with architectural wonders from every age *(see pp10–11)*.

3 Niguliste Church

Few places offer a more sumptuous feast of medieval art than Niguliste Church. Home to a collection of statues, altarpieces and church silverware, the church also houses Tallinn's single most valuable artistic treasure – Bernt Notke's *Danse Macabre* *(see pp12–13)*.

4 City Museum

The lives and times of Tallinners through the ages are thrown into sharp relief by this absorbing collection of artifacts and artworks. The Gothic museum building is an attraction in itself *(see pp14–15)*.

Preceding pages **Rooftops and church spires, Old Town**

5 The City Walls

The limestone walls and pinnacled towers of Tallinn's medieval fortifications remain one of the city's most unforgettable sights. They were built to save Tallinn from successive sieges in the 16th century *(see pp16–17)*.

Dome Church 6

Filled with grave memorials honouring the great and the good, Tallinn's main Lutheran cathedral is both a sculpture gallery as well as a place of worship *(see pp18–19)*.

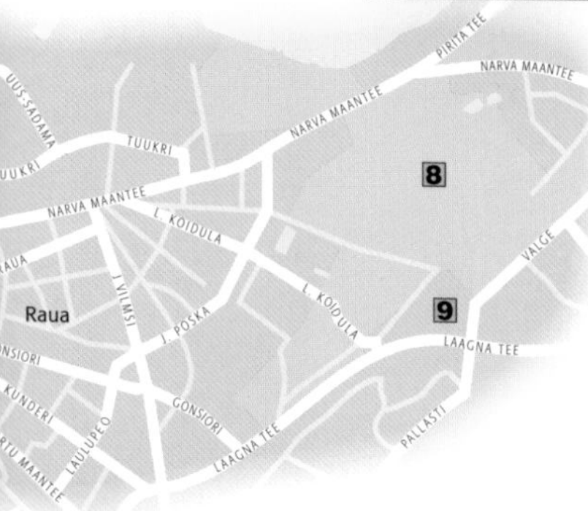

7 Museum of Occupations

A compelling account of Estonia's 20th-century misfortunes, this is one museum display that will linger in the memory for a very long time *(see pp20–21)*.

Kadriorg Park 8

Peter the Great's 18th-century pleasure gardens have survived to become Tallinn's best-loved park, boasting tree-shaded pathways, a huge children's playground and the city's most fascinating art museums *(see pp22–3)*.

9 KUMU

Estonia's National Art Museum is both a thrilling piece of contemporary architecture and an engrossing gallery collection, housing masterpieces by 20th century Estonian artists *(see pp26–9)*.

The Estonian Open-Air Museum 10

Ranged across a partly forested seaside park west of the town centre is this collection of traditional farm buildings. They were brought to Tallinn timber-by-timber from various Estonian provinces *(see pp30–31)*.

Town Hall Square and Around

Tallinn's Town Hall Square is the fulcrum around which all life in the Old Town revolves, playing host to a daily throng of office workers, shoppers and tourists. Originally a medieval market, the square is now lined with cafés and restaurants, whose parasol-covered terraces spill out onto the flagstones in summer. The most famous building on the square is the Gothic Town Hall itself, although medieval splendours also extend to the narrow alleyways branching off on either side, where high-gabled merchants' houses loom above the cobblestones.

Town Hall Square Market

Town Hall Square is peaceful in the early morning, when most cafés are yet to open.

The Kõrts Inn Krug *(see p85)* in the Town Hall provides a unique medieval setting.

- *Map J3*
- *Town Hall: Raekoja plats 1; 645 7900; Open 10am–4pm Mon–Sat Jul–Aug, Sep–Jun call ahead to arrange a visit; €2.90*
- *Town Hall Pharmacy: Raekoja plats 11; 631 4860; Open 10am–6pm Tue–Sat*
- *Church of the Holy Ghost: Pühavaimu 2; 644 1487; Open 9am–4pm Mon–Sat*
- *Museum of Photography: Raekoja tänav 4/6; 644 8767; Open 10:30am–6pm Thu–Tue Mar–Oct, 10am–5:30pm Thu–Mon Nov–Feb*
- *Kullo Gallery: Kuninga 6; 644 6873; Open 10am–6pm Tue–Sat; €0.50*
- *The Bishop's House: Kiriku plats 3*
- *The Pakkhoone: Vana turg 1*
- *The Gothic House: Raekoja plats 18; 644 5339*

Top 10 Features

1. The Town Hall
2. Town Council Chamber
3. Town Hall Tower
4. Town Hall Pharmacy
5. Church of the Holy Ghost
6. Museum of Photography
7. Kullo Gallery
8. The Bishop's House
9. The Pakkhoone
10. The Gothic House at Vanaturu kael 3

1 The Town Hall

The current Town Hall dates from 1404, although its origins lie at least a century earlier. Water spouts in the shape of dragons *(above)* add charm to the building's arcaded northern façade.

2 Town Council Chamber

Open to visitors in summer, the Town Council Chamber contains a beautiful wood-carved frieze of huntsmen and animals surrounded by a forest *(below)*.

3 Town Hall Tower

The slender octagonal tower that spears skywards from the Town Hall's eastern gable is its most striking feature. The weather vane at the tower's summit takes the form of a broad-hatted soldier known as Vana Toomas (Old Thomas).

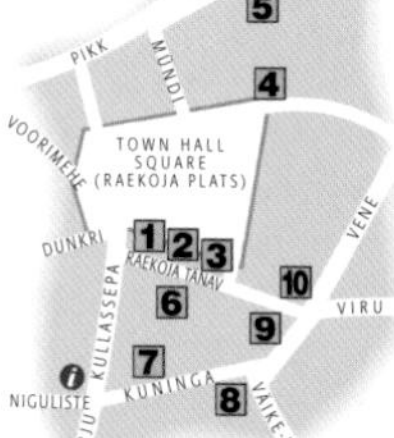

4 Town Hall Pharmacy

Dating from 1422, the Town Hall Pharmacy (Raeapteek) has a working trade counter at one end and a small museum at the other *(above)*.

5 Church of the Holy Ghost

This church is instantly recognizable by its stepped gable and slender white tower. The interior is a treasure trove of art, with a baroque-era gallery and a late-Gothic high altar.

6 Museum of Photography

The stone chambers of a 14th-century prison now provide an atmospheric home for the Museum of Photography *(right)*, with a collection featuring images of Tallinn past and present.

7 Kullo Gallery

The Kullo Gallery of children's art provides a rare opportunity to examine the interior of a typical merchant's house. On the first floor is the Prudentia Room, in which a baroque painting of the goddess of wisdom fills the ceiling.

8 The Bishop's House

Dating from the mid-14th century, the Bishop's House (Piiskopimaja) is famous for the portraits of Christ and the Evangelists placed in circular niches high up the façade.

9 The Pakkhoone

This bulky 17th-century building on Vanaturu kael is where foreign merchants once stored their wares, pending inspection by officials from the Town Hall.

10 The Gothic House at Vanaturu kael 3

Unarguably the most conspicuous building on Vanaturu kael, the "Matkamaja" (Traveller's House) is a late-Gothic structure. The loading hatch with a jutting crane on the top floor points to its former role as a merchant's home and storehouse *(right)*.

Vana Toomas

The Town Hall's Vana Toomas (Old Thomas) weather vane has been one of the city's best loved landmarks ever since the 16th century. According to urban legend, the original Toomas was a commoner who surprised Tallinn's upper classes by beating them fair and square in the city's annual archery contest. Toomas was rewarded with the job of town guard, subsequently serving as the inspiration for this memorial.

TOP 10 Along Pikk Street

Running through Tallinn's Old Town from north to south, Pikk (Long Street) *takes you past many of the city's most representative buildings. The street boasts particularly large numbers of the tall, pointed-roofed merchants' houses that lend Tallinn its unique Gothic character. Also found along Pikk are the palaces of Tallinn's medieval guilds, who once controlled the commercial life of the city. Nowadays Pikk is an excellent location in which to browse for souvenirs, its shops crammed with handmade chocolates, hand-woven textiles and other authentic crafts.*

Interior of Anneli Viik café

For delicious chocolates or a slice of fancy cake, head for the swanky Anneli Viik café *(see p85)* midway along the street.

- *Maritime Museum: Pikk 70; Map K2; 641 1408; Open 10am–6pm Wed–Sun; €4*
- *The Three Sisters: Pikk 71; Map K2*
- *Oleviste Church: Lai 50; Map J2; 641 2241; Open 10am–6pm Apr–Oct*
- *House of the Blackheads: Pikk 26; Map J3; 631 3199*
- *The Canute Guild: Pikk 20; 646 4704*
- *Draakoni House: Pikk 18; 646 4110; Open 11am–6pm Mon–Fri, 11am–5pm Sat*
- *The Great Guild: Pikk 17; Map J3; 641 1630*
- *Maiasmokk: Pikk 16; Map J3; 6464 079; Open 10am–6pm Thu–Tue; €5*

Top 10 Features

1. Maritime Museum
2. The Three Sisters
3. Oleviste Church
4. Former KGB Building
5. Roheline Turg
6. House of the Blackheads
7. The Canute Guild
8. Draakoni House
9. The Great Guild
10. Maiasmokk

1 Maritime Museum

Model ships, antique telescopes and other sea faring memorabilia are gathered together in the Old Town branch of the Maritime Museum. The museum is housed in the interior of a drum-shaped tower known as Fat Margaret *(see p16)*.

2 The Three Sisters

This trio of 15th-century houses represents Gothic Tallinn at its picturesque best. The southernmost of the sisters has a façade with arched and circular niches.

3 Oleviste Church

Towering above the Old Town's northern end, the Oleviste Church *(left)* is famous for its soaring steeple, which was the highest in the world when first built in 1500.

4 Former KGB Building

This 19th-century apartment block was once the HQ of the Soviet security department. There is little sign of its sinister role left.

5 Roheline Turg

One of the smallest green spaces in Tallinn, this park overlooks the junction of Pikk and Olevimägi. It was once the site of a vegetable market, hence its name, which means "Green Square". The dainty Orthodox chapel at the end of the park dates from 1909.

9 The Great Guild

Built in 1407 when the guild of Tallinn's merchants wielded considerable power, this building is an outstanding example of Tallinn Gothic *(below)*.

6 House of the Blackheads

Tallinn's most famous façade, the House of the Blackheads at Pikk 26 *(above)* is studded with reliefs by the city's most gifted 16th-century stonemason, Arent Passer. Particularly exquisite are the plaques portraying duelling knights just above the first floor windows.

7 The Canute Guild

This striking 19th-century mansion in English neo-Tudor style was once home to the Canute Guild, the association of artisans who took their name from King Canute IV, patron saint of Denmark. The building now serves as a dance theatre.

10 Maiasmokk

Site of a café for 200 years, Maiasmokk (Sweet Tooth) simply oozes olde-worlde charm with its old-fashioned, wood-panelled rooms. Famous for its marzipan since its establishment in 1864, Maiasmokk is a Tallinn institution. Sweet makers can be observed at work behind the counter of the café's sweet shop *(above)*.

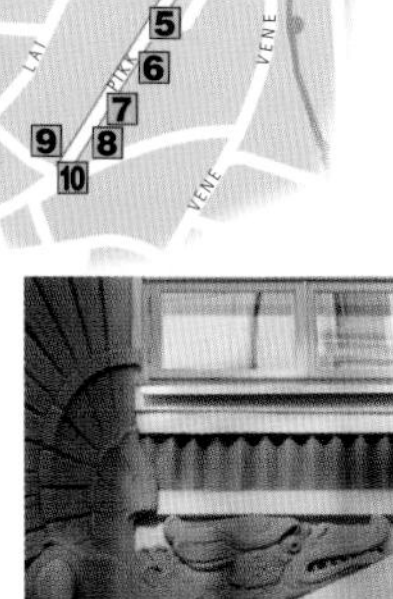

8 Draakoni House

Built in 1911, this fine Art Nouveau building now houses an art gallery. Draakoni House owes its name to the flamboyant façade decorations, with a pair of black-winged dragons *(above)* sprawling above the first floor windows.

The Brotherhood of the Blackheads

Founded in 1399, the Brotherhood of the Blackheads brought together the city's young single merchants – who as bachelors were considered not ready to join the ranks of the Great Guild. The Blackheads played a key role in the social life of the city, organizing tournaments, seasonal festivities and drinking bouts. They took their name from their patron, St Maurice, a Roman saint of North African origin who is traditionally portrayed as dark skinned.

Niguliste Church

Packed with ecclesiastical artworks, the Niguliste Church showcases Tallinn's medieval cultural heritage. Begun in the 13th century and dedicated to the patron of seafarers, it was damaged in the Soviet bombing raids of March 1944. After decades of restoration work the church reopened as a museum in 1984. It houses a rich collection of paintings, sculpture and silverware, while the church's organ sounds every afternoon on weekends, when recitals are held.

Statue of St Christopher

Illustration from the High Altar

Immediately south of the Niguliste Church is an innovatively designed stretch of park, featuring a terraced garden and benches in the shape of sun loungers.

At the top end of the park stands a small café in an angular glass pavilion. It serves good coffee and tempting cakes.

- *Map J4*
- *Niguliste 3*
- *644 9903*
- *Open 10am–5pm Wed–Sun*
- *€3.20*
- *Organ concerts at 4pm Sat and Sun*
- *www.ekm.ee*

Top 10 Features

1. Altar of the Brotherhood of the Blackheads
2. The Silver Chamber
3. The Bogislaus Rosen Altar Screen
4. The High Altar
5. The Altar of the Holy Kin
6. The Baptistery
7. The Passion Altar
8. The Statue of St Christopher
9. The Danse Macabre
10. Tombstones in St Matthew's Chapel

1 Altar of the Brotherhood of the Blackheads

The Brotherhood of the Blackheads were eager contributors to Tallinn's churches. Painted by an anonymous Bruges artist in 1490, the altar's central panel depicts a radiant, red-robed Virgin Mary flanked by saints.

2 The Silver Chamber

Tallinn's guilds were keen collectors of ornate silverware, as this display aptly demonstrates *(below)*. Many of the ceremonial tankards on show were made by local artisans.

3 The Bogislaus Rosen Altar Screen

Commissioned by wealthy burgher Bogislaus Rosen in 1665, this altar screen features family emblems of Rosen's two wives, entwined in carved foliage.

4 The High Altar

Completed by Lübeck artist Hermen Rode in 1481, the High Altar is a complex and dynamic work of art. The central scenes are flanked by enormous hinged panels decorated with scenes from the lives of St Nicholas and St Victor.

9 The Danse Macabre

Filling one wall of St Matthew's Chapel, this late 15th-century painting is a deliciously ghoulish reminder of life's transience. Painted by Lübeck artist Bernt Notke, it shows seven skeletal figures leading five humans (including a pope) in a macabre dance *(right)*.

5 The Altar of the Holy Kin

Although only a central fragment of this late-Gothic altarpiece survives *(above)*, the painted statues and reliefs provide ample proof of the three-dimensional composition skills of the itinerant artists of the time.

7 The Passion Altar

A haunting Crucifixion scene set against a brooding city-scape filled with turrets, the Passion Altar (1515) was painted by Adriaen Isenbrant of Bruges, another north-European artist lured by the wealth of Tallinn's churches.

8 The Statue of St Christopher

Carved by Tobias Heinze in 1624, this life-sized wooden statue was used to support the church pulpit, which explains the Saint's stooping posture. The saint's expressive features make this an outstanding example of the carver's art.

10 Tombstones in St Matthew's Chapel

As if to underline the message of Notke's painting, the floor of St Matthew's Chapel is covered with carved tombstones. The Niguliste Church was a popular last resting place for Tallinn's families, and many slabs are adorned with carved crests.

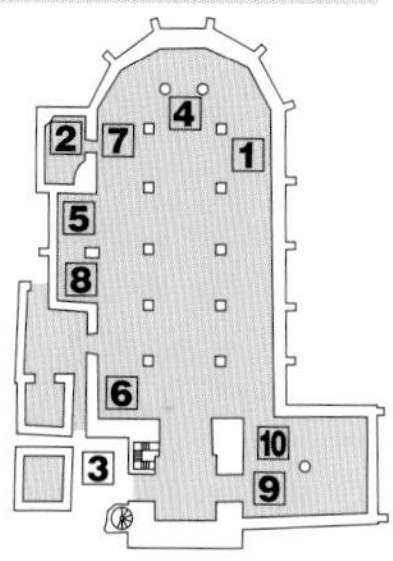

6 The Baptistery

A curious structure that looks like a modern-day gazebo *(below)*, this octagonal wooden baptistery by baroque sculptor Christian Ackerman is topped with statuettes of the apostles.

Dance of Death

The Dance of Death was a popular subject for church paintings throughout 15th century Europe. They almost always showed frisky skeletons leading away prominent members of society – kings, bishops and merchants – in order to drive home the message that death will catch up with you whoever you are. The painters were full of visual humour: the skeletons always look more agile than their leaden-footed human partners.

TOP 10 City Museum

For a true insight into Tallinn's hard-headed mercantile nature, look no further than the City Museum. It is clear from the historical coins, strongboxes and weights and measures on display that trade lies at the heart of the city's historical experience. The town's business success helped maintain a rich and diverse culture as can be seen from the paintings, manuscripts and church treasures exhibited. The museum itself is located in the typically tall and narrow house of a medieval merchant, with exhibits spread over four floors.

Exterior of the City Museum

Guided tours in English and other languages are available by prior appointment. Call in advance on 6155 180.

There is a small café and gift shop on the top floor of the museum, offering a lovely view of the street scene below.

- *Map K3*
- *Vene 17*
- *6155 180*
- *Open 10:30am–6pm Closed Tue*
- *€3.20*
- *www.linnamuuseum.ee*

Top 10 Features

1. Scale Model of Tallinn in 1825
2. The Evald Aav Room
3. Veronika's Kerchief by Clawes van der Sittow
4. Balthasar Russow's Livonian Chronicle of 1578
5. Scale Model of the Huck House
6. Portrait of Queen Christina of Sweden
7. Propaganda Posters
8. The Baltic Cog
9. The 19th Century Room
10. Olympic Souvenirs

1 Scale Model of Tallinn in 1825

This model *(below)* shows Tallinn at a time when most of its fortifications were still intact. Many of the angular jutting bastions visible here were demolished in the mid-19th century, to be replaced by parkland or highways.

2 The Evald Aav Room

Evald Aav (1900–1939) wrote the first Estonian opera, *Vikerlased* (The Vikings), in 1928. This re-creation of Aav's living room contains the Art-Deco influenced furniture that was popular with Tallinn's inter-war intelligentsia *(right)*.

3 Veronika's Kerchief by Clawes van der Sittow

Painted in 1460 by Clawes van der Sittow, father of Tallinn's celebrated 16th-century artist Michael Sittow, this image of Jesus on the handkerchief of St Veronica once adorned the end of a bench in Tallinn's Town Hall.

4 Balthasar Russow's Livonian Chronicle of 1578

Penned by the pastor at Tallinn's Church of the Holy Ghost, the Livonian Chronicle describes Estonian life during the 16th century. A pioneering piece of historical writing, it is also a beautiful example of book production.

5 Scale Model of the Huck House

A typical 15th-century merchant's dwelling *(left)*, the Huck House featured kitchens and living space on the ground floor, while merchandise – hauled up by a crane protruding from the gable – was stored on the floors above.

6 Portrait of Queen Christina of Sweden

Tallinn was under Swedish rule from 1561 to 1710, a period remembered as the "Good Swedish Times" by Estonians who appreciated rational government. This painting by Johan Bannier is a fine example of the portraiture of the time.

7 Propaganda Posters

Caught between the competing ambitions of Nazi Germany and the Soviet Union, Estonians spent the 1940s being bombarded with propaganda by one occupier or another. This atmosphere has been admirably captured by this display *(main image)*.

8 The Baltic Cog

A robust cargo vessel that could withstand choppy seas, the cog was the workhorse of Baltic trade. Tallinn's port would once have been full of these vessels, shipping Baltic furs and timber to the ports of Germany and Holland.

9 The 19th Century Room

The 19th century brought modern industry, railway connections and tourism to Tallinn, an era of change summed up by this display of period costumes and furnishings *(below)*.

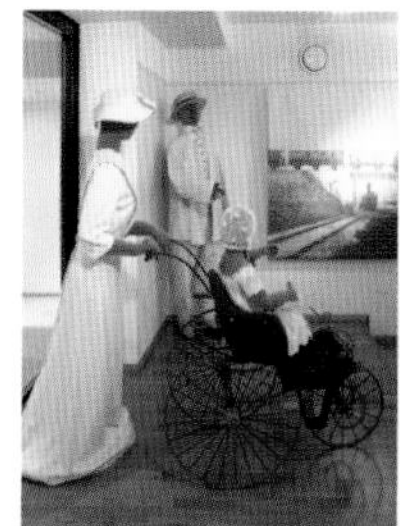

10 Olympic Souvenirs

The yachting events of the 1980 Olympics took place in Tallinn, producing a rash of Olympic-related souvenirs. The "Tallinn 1980" logo is one of the few reminders of the Soviet era that still inspires a degree of nostalgia.

The Hanseatic League

Tallinn owed its mercantile success to its membership of the Hanseatic League, a 13th-century association of north-European port cities. The league was like a common market, allowing merchants to trade on equal terms. Its influence began to fade in the 15th century when the Hanseatic cities began competing for the same markets.

TOP 10 The City Walls

Although no longer girdling the city in an unbroken circle, Tallinn's medieval walls still boast some remarkably well-preserved stretches, complete with a skyline-defining collection of red-roofed medieval towers. The walls reached their greatest extent in the 16th century, when they linked an integrated fortification system comprising over 40 towers and an outer moat. Twenty towers and gates remain today, a handful of which have been restored and made accessible to visitors.

Müürivahe market

Visiting Tallinn's surviving towers usually involves negotiating steep and narrow staircases – a normal level of agility and sturdy footwear are required.

- *Map J2*
- *Fat Margaret: Pikk 70; Map K2; 641 1408; Open 10am–6pm Wed–Sun; €4*
- *Kiek-in-de-kök: Komandandi 2; Map H4; 644 6686; Open 10:30am–6pm Tue–Sun Mar–Oct, 10am–5:30pm Nov–Feb; €4.50*
- *Viru Gate: Viru tänav; Map K4*

Top 10 Features

1. Tornide väljak
2. Müürivahe
3. Fat Margaret
4. The Horse Mill
5. Kiek-in-de-kök
6. The Epping Tower
7. The Nun's Tower
8. Tallitorn
9. Hellemann Tower
10. Viru Gate

1 Tornide väljak

The best view of Tallinn's surviving fortifications is the one from Tornide väljak (Tower Square) on the Old Town's western side. From here you can look back on a 500-metre (1,640-ft) long stretch of wall that takes in eight well-preserved towers *(main image)*.

2 Müürivahe

North of Viru Gate, the narrow cobbled alley called Müürivahe (between-the-walls) runs behind a long stretch of surviving wall, punctuated by stocky towers. The alley is famous for its souvenir stalls that specialize in traditional woolly jumpers.

3 Fat Margaret

Built in the 16th century to serve as a cannon platform and ammunition depot, this barrel-shaped bastion *(below)* studded with gun ports today provides an atmospheric home to the Estonian Maritime Museum.

4 The Horse Mill

This enigmatic cylindrical building on the corner of Tolli and Lai streets was built in the 16th century to house a horse-powered water pump. The pump's main purpose was to fill the city's defensive moat during times of siege.

5 Kiek-in-de-kök

Built in the 16th century to provide a fire platform for Tallinn's heavy cannons *(above)*, Kiek-in-de-kök (peek into the kitchen) refers to the views from the cannon ports of domestic interiors below.

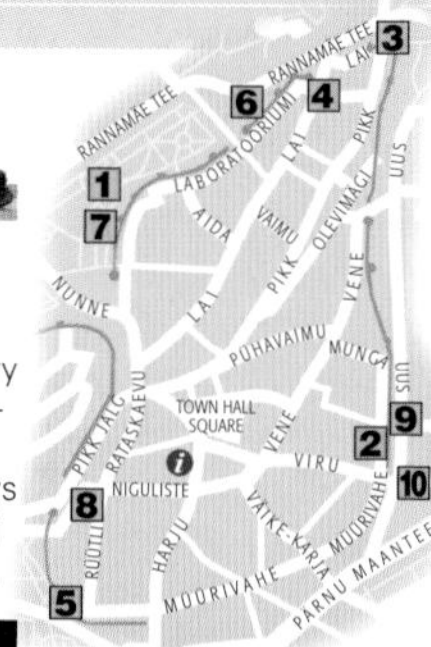

6 The Epping Tower

This sturdy half cylinder gets its name from city alderman Tideman Epping, who supervised its construction in the 1370s. Ascend the tower to see exhibits *(above)* on the history of Tallinn's fortifications.

7 The Nun's Tower

The Nun's Tower (Nunnatorn) provides access to a restored stretch of the City Walls on the western side of the Old Town.

8 Tallitorn

Once a prison for minor offenders, the Tallitorn now provides access to a short stretch of wall. Below stretches a park known as the Danish King's Garden – a reference to the Danish defeat of the pagan Estonians here in 1219.

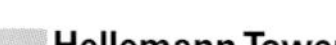

9 Hellemann Tower

Midway along Müürivahe, the stocky Hellemann Tower houses an art gallery and provides access to the wall's parapet. Peek through crossbow holes towards Tallinn's modern down-town districts to the east.

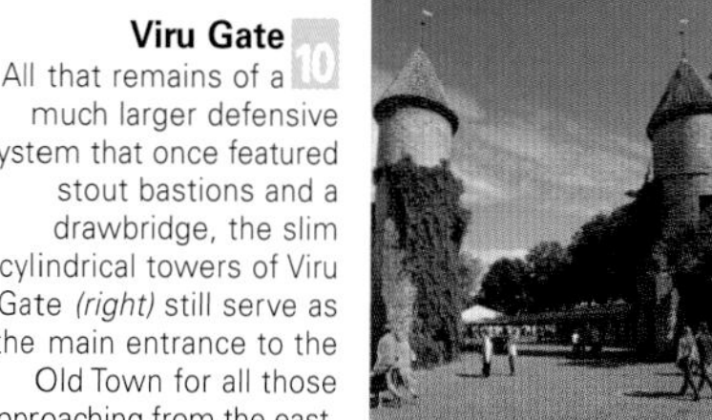

10 Viru Gate

All that remains of a much larger defensive system that once featured stout bastions and a drawbridge, the slim cylindrical towers of Viru Gate *(right)* still serve as the main entrance to the Old Town for all those approaching from the east.

History of the Walls

Built from distinctive grey limestone, Tallinn's first stone fortifications were erected in 1265. Strengthened in 1310 by King Erik VI of Denmark, they underwent major expansion in the 15th century, when the cone-topped towers took shape. Towards the end of the 16th century, the development of artillery led to the construction of towers like Kiek-in-de-kök and Fat Margaret, both of which were broad enough to hold a battery of cannon.

Top 10 Dome Church

Dating from the Danish conquest in 1219, and quite possibly the oldest church on the Estonian mainland, the Cathedral of St Mary the Virgin, or Dome Church, (Toomkirik, *in Estonian, is a corruption of the German* Domkirche) *retains the look of a dainty medieval parish church. The interior, however, boasts an outstanding collection of funerary monuments reflecting sculptural styles from Renaissance to Neo-Classical. Those interested in baroque art will find much to enjoy, especially the church's spectacular collection of 16th-century armorial shields.*

Luscher & Matiesen outdoor café

A five-minute stroll northeast from the church takes you to the Kohtuotsa Viewing Platform. It offers a panorama of Tallinn's Old Town.

The Luscher & Matiesen outdoor café *(see p73)*, right beside the Kohtuotsa viewing platform, is a relaxing place for a drink.

- *Map H3*
- *Toomkooli 6*
- *644 4140*
- *Open 9am–5pm Tue–Sun*

Top 10 Features

1. Armorial Shields
2. The Greig Tomb
3. Family Boxes
4. The Church Organ
5. The Uexküll Tomb
6. The Pontus de la Gardie Tomb
7. Grave Slabs
8. The High Altar
9. The von Krusenstern Tomb
10. The Pulpit

1 Armorial Shields

These wooden shields *(above)*, bearing the crests of Tallinn's leading families, feature delicately carved leaves and three-dimensional figures of knights and animals.

2 The Greig Tomb

The tomb of Russian Admiral Samuel Greig is a wonderful example of Neo-Classical sculpture, featuring statues of grieving females and winged angels.

3 Family Boxes

Positioned beside the choir are pews of two of Tallinn's most powerful families, the Manteuffels and the Patkuls. Enclosed in glass, these pews *(above)* are separated from the rest of the congregation by a stairway.

4 The Church Organ

The organ *(left)* is housed in a 19th-century Neo-Gothic case that is flamboyantly decorated with branching pinnacles and vegetal swirls.

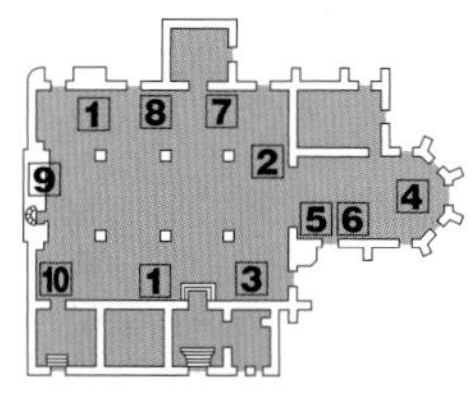

5 The Uexküll Tomb

Occupying the choir is the grave slab of Otto von Uexküll *(right)*, one of the masterpieces of Tallinn's leading 16th-century stonemason, Arent Passer. Uexküll is shown in relief form, clad in a full suit of armour.

6 The Pontus de la Gardie Tomb

Passer's other masterpiece is the tomb of Pontus de la Gardie, the Swedish general who defeated Ivan the Terrible's troops at Narva in 1578.

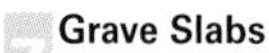

7 Grave Slabs

The church floor is covered with the numbered burial plots of Tallinn's leading families or guilds. Most immediately recognizable is the plot belonging to the guild of cobblers – their slab is decorated with a relief of a thigh-length boot.

8 The High Altar

The Cathedral's High Altar incorporates a fine Crucifixion painted by Eduard von Gebhard. It is framed by an elaborate sculptural ensemble, including Christ and the Evangelists, the work of Christian Ackerman.

9 The von Krusenstern Tomb

Close to the Greig Tomb is a monument to Johann von Krusenstern, the Tsarist naval officer who circumnavigated the globe in 1806. In clear reference to the admiral's voyages of discovery, the tomb is decorated with figures wearing ethnic costumes.

10 The Pulpit

Mounted halfway up a pillar at the entrance to the choir is Christian Ackerman's ornate Baroque pulpit *(above)*, with statuettes of the apostles interspersed with corkscrew-shaped columns. The pulpit's canopy is topped by a lively cluster of cherubs.

Admiral Samuel Greig (1736–88)

A Scottish-born officer in the British navy, Samuel Greig was offered a post in the Russian imperial fleet and soon rose to the position of captain. Victory against the Turks at the Battle of Chesma in 1770 saw his elevation to admiral. Greig came down with a fever while campaigning against the Swedes in 1788 and died in Tallinn harbour. Empress Catherine the Great accorded him a state funeral in the Dome Church.

Museum of Occupations

Despite the fact that Estonia was on paper an equal republic in the USSR, the Soviet period has always been regarded by Estonians as an illegal occupation by an imperial power. Housed in a boldly contemporary glass wedge, the Museum of Occupations presents an informative and moving account of Estonia's experience of Soviet rule. Besides providing a sobering account of State persecution, the display also reveals the absurd side of a system that left Eastern Europe technologically backward in relation to the West.

Hirvepark

Around the corner from the museum is the Hirvepark, one of central Tallinn's most attractive green spaces and the perfect location for a stroll or a picnic.

A five minute walk to the south of the museum is Vabaduse väljak, where Kuku café has chairs and tables spread out over the flagstones.

- *Map H5*
- *Toompea 8*
- *668 0250*
- *Open 11am–6pm Tue–Sun*
- *€2*
- *www.okupatsioon.ee*

Top 10 Features

1. Refugee Boat
2. Prison Doors
3. Suitcases
4. Viktor Kingissepp
5. Popular Magazines
6. German Army Uniform
7. Forest Brothers
8. Letter Steamer
9. Juku Computer
10. Film Clips and Newsreels

1 Refugee Boat

Towards the end of World War II, many Estonians fled the country before the arrival of the Soviet Red Army. This wooden fishing boat *(main image)* was used by Estonians from the island of Hiiumaa to reach the Swedish island of Gotland.

2 Prison Doors

Standing in mute testimony to those interrogated and tortured in KGB prisons is this line of metal cell doors *(left)*, taken from several locations throughout Estonia.

3 Suitcases

Arranged in piles throughout the museum, these suitcases *(right)* act as powerful reminders of the mass deportations that were used by the Soviet occupiers to break the will of the Estonian popular resistance. The main waves of deportation took place in June 1941 and March 1949.

4 Viktor Kingissepp

Among the statues in the museum basement are several portrayals of Viktor Kingissepp (1888–1922). The Estonian communist agitator *(left)*, hailed as a revolutionary hero during Soviet occupation, was executed by the inter-war Estonian state.

5 Popular Magazines

When the Soviets took over Estonia in June 1940 they found a developed country saturated with consumer goods and sophisticated media. Stylish fashion magazines *(below)* were immediately subjected to political control and used to spread the Marxist message.

6 German Army Uniform

Following a year of Soviet occupation, Estonia was invaded by Nazi Germany in June 1941. Estonia was incorporated into the German-ruled province of Ostland and any opposition was ruthlessly suppressed.

7 Forest Brothers

The "Forest Brothers" were guerrillas who fought against the authorities after Soviet reoccupation of Estonia in 1944. They were forced to surrender in the mid-1950s.

8 Letter Steamer

Looking rather like a domestic clothes iron, this steamer *(above)* for opening letters enabled security operatives to intercept and read the mail of Estonian citizens.

9 Juku Computer

The Juku school computer shows how Estonia, always one of the more developed republics in the Soviet Union, attempted to keep up with the West.

10 Film Clips and Newsreels

The museum display makes full use of film and video. Particularly inspiring are TV images from the late 1980s, when the "Singing Revolution" successfully challenged the communist establishment.

The Molotov-Ribbentrop Pact

The fate of independent Estonia was effectively sealed by the Molotov-Ribbentrop Pact of August 1939, a secret agreement between Nazi Germany and the Soviet Union to carve up northeastern Europe between them. The Soviets occupied the Baltic states in June 1940. Public discussion of the pact was banned during the Soviet period and publication of its terms became a hugely symbolic issue for the Estonian independence movement in the late 1980s.

Top 10 Kadriorg Park

The leafy landscaped park of Kadriorg is where Tallinners come to stretch their legs and escape the bustle of the city centre. With a trio of unmissable art museums and a wealth of historical monuments, it's a magnet for sightseers too. Kadriorg started out as the pleasure garden of Russian Emperor Peter the Great who conquered Tallinn in 1710 and resolved to build a palace here for his wife, Empress Catherine I. It is from her that the park gets its name: Kadriorg is Estonian for "Catherine's Valley".

Tram from Viru väljak to Kadriorg Park

The easiest way to get to Kadriorg is by tram no.1 or no. 3 from Viru väljak. Both drop you at the main southwestern entrance to the park.

Have a snack at the Park Café *(see p101)* just inside Kadriorg Park's western gate, where you can enjoy tea and cakes under the trees.

• Map C5
• Kadriorg Palace Art Museum: Weizenbergi 37; 606 6403; Open 10am–5pm Tue–Sun; €4.20 • Peter the Great's House: Mäekalda 2; 601 3136; Open 10am–6pm Tue–Sun; €1.92 • Eduard Vilde Museum: Roheline aas 3; 601 3181; Open 11am–6pm Wed–Mon; €1.92 • Park Museum: Weizenbergi 26; 601 3183; Open 10am–5pm Wed–Sun • Mikkel Museum: Weizenbergi 28; 601 5844; Open 10am–5pm Wed–Sun; €2.20

Top 10 Features

1. Kadriorg Palace Art Museum
2. KUMU Art Museum
3. Peter the Great's House
4. The Rusalka Memorial
5. Eduard Vilde Museum
6. Swan Lake
7. Park Museum
8. Children's Play Park
9. The Mikkel Museum
10. Kreutzwald Memorial

1 Kadriorg Palace Art Museum

Occupying the palace built for Peter the Great by Niccolò Michetti *(above)*, this museum has a collection of old masters. The baroque interiors boast flamboyant stuccowork.

2 KUMU Art Museum

Opened in 2006, KUMU's limestone walls emerge from a natural hillside *(below)*. The exhibits follow the evolution of Estonian modern art from its 19th-century beginnings to the present day *(see pp26–7)*.

3 Peter the Great's House

This one-storey cottage is where Peter the Great lived from 1714 to 1716, supervising the administration of his newly conquered Baltic provinces. Antique wooden furnishings convey a convincing sense of period.

The Rusalka Memorial 4

Featuring an imperious-looking angel wielding a gleaming cross, this is one of Tallinn's most stirring examples of public sculpture *(right)*. It was erected in honour of Russian warship *Rusalka*, which sank with all hands during a storm in 1893.

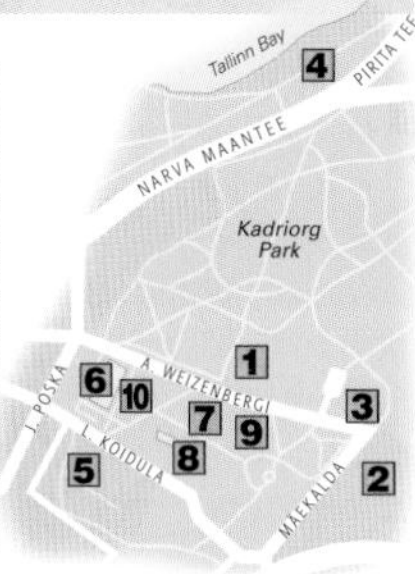

5 Eduard Vilde Museum

The home of novelist Eduard Vilde (1865–1933) is now a museum. The well-preserved interiors shed light on the domestic tastes of the 1930s.

6 Swan Lake

The aptly named Swan Lake is a rectangular stretch of water popular with waterfowl *(main image)*. Sitting on an island in the middle of the lake is a delightful domed gazebo.

7 Park Museum

Housed in a wooden sentry pavilion built during the reign of Tsar Nicholas I, the Park Museum's collection of horticultural plans and sepia photographs reveals how Kadriorg Park took shape over the years.

8 Children's Play Park

Right in the middle of Kadriog Park is Tallinn's biggest children's play area *(left)*. The seesaws, swings and sandpits here induce a constant buzz of activity.

9 The Mikkel Museum

Amassed over a lifetime by antiques dealer Johannes Mikkel, this wide-ranging collection takes in Chinese porcelain *(right)*, European paintings and rare prints – including Estonia's only Rembrandt.

10 Kreutzwald Memorial

F. R. Kreutzwald's towering status in Estonian literature is aptly expressed by this larger-than-life statue. The plinth is decorated with scenes from *Kalevipoeg*, the national epic poem he compiled in 1857 *(see p35)*.

Empress Catherine I

Empress Catherine I of Russia began life as Marta Skavronska, a Polish-Latvian serving girl. Taken to St Petersburg by General Sheremetev, her beauty entranced the Russian court. Peter the Great secretly married her in 1707. Converting to Orthodoxy and taking the name Catherine, she ruled alone as Empress following Peter's death in 1725.

Left **Port of Tallinn by Alexandar Bogolyubov** Centre **Main Hall** Right **Exhibit, Silver Chamber**

TOP 10 Kadriorg Palace Art Museum

Beauty Directed by Prudence

1 The Main Hall

Preserving its original decoration from the time of Peter the Great, the Main Hall is a three-dimensional celebration of imperial power. Delicately stuccoed double-headed eagles (symbols of Holy Russia) glare down from above the ornate fireplaces.

2 Italian Vases from Scavona Town

Highlights of the palace's rich porcelain collection include these two 19th-century vases from Scavona, decorated with scenes of ancient battles.

3 The National Room

Dating from the inter-war period, the National Room contains furnishings mixing 20th-century style with folk motifs. Most eyecatching is Jakob Jõgi's drinks cabinet, adorned with reliefs illustrating the national epic, *Kalevipoeg* *(see p35)*.

4 Beauty Directed by Prudence

Austrian-born Angelica Kauffmann was one of the most popular painters of the early 18th century. This painting, commissioned by rich London widow Ann Bryer, was reproduced by many print-makers, becoming one of the most widely-distributed images in 19th-century Europe.

5 The Silver Chamber

This glittering collection of bowls, goblets and tankards concentrates on the output of Baltic silversmiths of the 16th to 19th centuries. The collection

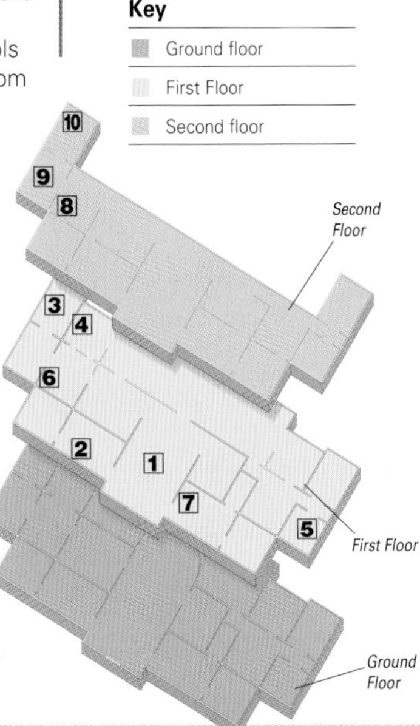

Diana and Actaeon

The Main Hall in Kadriorg Palace is dominated by a large ceiling painting illustrating the myth of Diana and Actaeon. According to legend, the Goddess of Hunting caught Actaeon secretly watching her while bathing and exacted revenge by transforming him into a stag and setting her dogs on him. The painting is intended as an allegory of Peter the Great's victories against Sweden, with Actaeon symbolizing the unfortunate Swedish King Charles XII – humiliatingly defeated after his impudent attack on Russia.

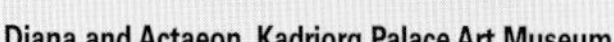

Diana and Actaeon, Kadriorg Palace Art Museum

also includes rare pieces from England and Russia, including a fruit bowl by St Petersburg jewellers Fabergé.

6 Portrait of Peter the Great

Completed by an anonymous artist soon after Peter's conquest of Tallinn, this imposing portrait surrounds the Russian emperor in symbols of majesty and power. Ships of the Russian fleet are pictured in the background.

7 Lady in Black by Bartholomew van der Helst

Portraitist van der Helst was much in demand in 17th-century Netherlands. This striking picture of a society lady provides an insight into the fashions of the time, with the subject clad in black silks and holding an ostrich-feather fan.

8 Port of Tallinn by Alexandar Bogolyubov

St Petersburg-educated Bogolyubov's maritime landscape shows how little Tallinn's Old Town skyline has changed since the 19th century – although the tall masts of the sailing ships have now been replaced by the funnels of Helsinki-Tallinn ferries.

9 Soldier's Tale by Ilya Repin

Russia's greatest 19th-century painter Ilya Repin (1844–1930) is represented by this one small canvas depicting a group of conscripts sharing a funny story. Repin sought to capture the character of the Russian people through these snapshots of life.

Soldier's Tale by Ilya Repin

10 Propagandist Porcelain

The Soviet Union initially embraced contemporary artists, allowing modernism to appear in all kinds of unlikely places. These dinner plates produced by the Lomonosov Porcelain Factory are outstanding examples of how constructivist art was applied to domestic design.

TOP 10 KUMU Modern Art Museum

Opened in 2006, KUMU Modern Art Museum is both the home of Estonia's national art collection and the leading exhibition space for international touring exhibitions – often with a decidedly contemporary edge. The building itself is breathtaking, built into a grassy ridge at the eastern edge of Kadriorg Park. Designed by Finnish architect Pekka Vapaavuori and making full use of the local limestone, it is an audaciously contemporary building that blends in well with its natural surroundings.

Interior of KUMU Café

The easiest way to reach KUMU is by taking tram no. 1 or 3 to Kadriorg and then walking through Kadriorg Park ***(see pp22–3).*** **Alternatively, take bus no. 31, 67 or 68 to the KUMU stop on Laagna tee. The museum is immediately below the bus stop.**

Wedged into the glassy western façade of the building, KUMU's chic café is the perfect place to take a breather ***(see p101).***

- *Map C5*
- *Weizenbergi 34*
- *602 6000*
- *Open 11am–6pm, Tue–Sun*
- *€5.50*
- *www.ekm.ee*

Top 10 Features

1. The Atrium
2. Composition with a Clock
3. The Imprecation of Lorelei by the Monks
4. Installation by Villu Jaanisoo
5. Konrad Mägi
6. Young Communist Workers
7. Surprise
8. Stream
9. Lenin
10. Top-floor Exhibition Galleries

1 The Atrium

The crescent-shaped nature of the main building is revealed only on entering the Atrium *(above)*. Gracefully curving walls loom above, with the first floor galleries reached via a sloping ramp.

2 Composition with a Clock

Estonian artists of the 1950s explored abstract art, even though such pictures were considered decadent to be exhibited officially. This collage by Kaja Kärner was made for private display only.

3 The Imprecation of Lorelei by the Monks

Covering an entire wall, this huge canvas *(below)* by Johann Köler was completed for his solo exhibition in Vienna in 1889.

4 Installation by Villu Jaanisoo

Contemporary artist Jaanisoo collected over 150 busts by Estonian sculptors through the ages, placing them all in this wedge-shaped chamber *(above)*. Accompanied by a soundtrack of babbling voices, it is an unusual lesson in Estonian cultural history.

6 Young Communist Workers

Already a leading painter in the 1920s and 30s, Adamson-Eric was an enthusiastic communist for the first few years of the Soviet occupation although he later became disillusioned. *Young Communist Workers* is a great example of the politically committed, socialist-realist art of the 1950s.

8 Stream

Communist policy towards the arts softened in the 1960s, and sculptors like Edgar Viies were allowed to experiment with unconventional forms. Describing himself as a "floating semi-abstractionist", Viies still came in for stern criticism from the party ideologists.

9 Lenin

A most ambiguous picture is this piece by Ilmar Malin (1924–94), who mixes surrealism, pop art and Soviet propaganda to disconcerting effect.

10 Top-floor Exhibition Galleries

Hosting a range of contemporary exhibitions, the top floor galleries *(above)* are a good place to check out the current state of Estonian art.

5 Konrad Mägi

KUMU devotes more space to Mägi than any other Estonian painter. His post-impressionist canvasses of the local countryside are among the most evocative Estonian landscapes ever produced.

7 Surprise

Timoleon von Neff (1804–76) was one of the first painters to treat Estonians as dignified subjects fit for art. *Surprise* shows country girls wearing traditional Estonian dresses of the time *(above)*.

Johann Köler (1826–99)

Born into a peasant family, Johann Köler was Estonia's first professionally trained painter. He travelled to St Petersburg to seek work painting street signs, eventually winning a place at the city's prestigious Art Academy. On graduating, Köler travelled throughout Europe to perfect his own realist style before returning to St Petersburg as a teacher. As well as being an in-demand portrait painter, Köler was also a social activist, promoting Estonian interests within the Tsarist Empire.

Left **Norwegian Landscape** Centre **Swimming the Horses** Right **At the Window**

Top 10 Modernist Paintings at KUMU

1 Rest on the Flight to Egypt

Münich-educated Kristjan Raud (1863–1943) was one of the first artists to introduce elements of impressionism and symbolism into Estonian art, setting the tone for the next generation of painters. Also a prolific book illustrator, Raud went on to exert a profound influence on Estonian graphic art.

2 Portrait of Irmgard Menning

Nikolai Triik (1884–1940) led the life of a starving young artist in Paris' Montmartre, returning to Estonia with a western urban sensibility. His portraits aim for psychological depth as well as physical accuracy. Triik's landscapes, also on display in KUMU museum, are highly regarded.

3 Norwegian Landscape with Pine

A companion of Triik in Paris, Konrad Mägi spent several years in Norway developing a highly individual, colour-saturated style of landscape painting. Never before had the north-European countryside been painted with such vibrancy and verve. Mägi's visit to Norway had a major influence on the Estonian island landscapes painted after the artist returned home.

4 Linda Carrying a Stone

Estonian folk themes remained a constant source of inspiration for Estonian artists. Oskar Kallis (1892–1918) was one of many who used Art Nouveau-inspired techniques to illustrate episodes from *Kalevipoeg*, the Estonian national epic.

Linda Carrying a Stone

5 Portrait of Elvi Gailit

Returning to Estonia, Mägi continued to paint restless and dizzy landscapes. However, he was also a fine portraitist, incorporating Art Nouveau and expressionist styles into his pictures.

6 Self Portrait

Jaan Vahtra (1882–1947) was profoundly influenced

Top 10 Facts about Konrad Mägi

1. Born in southern Estonia in 1878.
2. Enrolled in Tartu drawing school in 1899.
3. Went to St Petersburg to study under Estonian artist Amandus Adamson in 1903.
4. Moved to Paris in 1907.
5. Painted the first of his Fauvist-inspired landscapes in 1908.
6. Mägi's first one-man show took place in Norway in 1910.
7. Returned to Estonia to become a teacher, 1912.
8. Travelled to Saaremaa in 1913, where he painted some of his most famous landscapes.
9. Became a director of the new Pallas Art School in Tartu in 1919.
10. Died in Tartu in 1925.

Konrad Mägi

Like most of Estonia's modern artists, Konrad Mägi (1878–1925) wanted to explore the Estonian character, simultaneously making best use of the avant-garde ideas coming from Western Europe and Russia. Heading for Paris with colleagues Jaan Koort and Nikolai Triik, he borrowed freely from the French post-impressionists and the Fauves. Returning to Estonia in 1912, Mägi went through a decade of feverish creativity. His Estonian landscapes, bursting with bright colour, present the country in a way that has never been seen before or since.

Landscape, Tartu, Viljandi Road

by the European avant-garde and was at the forefront of the Estonian arts scene in the 1920s and 30s. This self-portrait by Vahtra exemplifies his constant search for a consummate blend of cubist and expressionist styles.

7 Two Ladies

Closely associated with Vahtra and his search for a synthesis of avant-garde styles, Felix Randell (1901–77) was a master of the post-cubist painting of the Art Deco age.

8 At the Window

Arnold Akberg (1894–1984) went further than any other Estonian artist in his search for pure form, taking his inspiration from the architect Le Corbusier as well as from the abstract painters of the European avant-garde.

9 Head

A colleague of Vahtra and Akberg, and in many ways exploring similar territory, Henrik Olvi (1894–1972) produced some of inter-war Estonia's most striking sculptures.

10 Swimming the Horses

Paul Burman (1888–1934) was another of the Estonian artists who lived as a Bohemian in Paris prior to World War I. He abandoned the avant-garde in the years that followed, seeking beauty in animals and nature instead.

The Estonian Open-Air Museum

Ranged across parkland in the seaside suburb of Rocca al Mare, the Estonian Open-Air Museum brings together more than 100 traditional buildings from all over the country. All the structures on display are authentic, having been dismantled in their home villages and reassembled here for conservation purposes. The interiors contain traditional furnishings, and rural handicrafts are demonstrated on summer weekends. The buildings are spread over a large area with plenty of meadow and forest in between, making it a delightful place for a lengthy stroll.

People cycling around the museum grounds

One of the most enjoyable ways to explore the museum is by bike. A range of good-quality bicycles can be hired from a pavilion next door to the museum entrance.

The Kolu Kõrts tavern in the centre of the museum offers traditional Estonian snacks and a full range of drinks *(see p101)*.

- *Map A1*
- *Vabaõhumuuseumi tee 12*
- *654 9100*
- *Bus 21 or 21B from the Balti Jaam train station*
- *Farmsteads open 10am–6pm May–Sep; 10am–5pm Oct–Apr*
- *€6 (May–Sep); €3 (Oct–Apr)*
- *Guided tours can be booked on 654 9100*
- *www.evm.ee*

Top 10 Features

1. Sassi-Jaani Farmstead
2. The Köstriaseme Farmstead
3. Kolu Kõrts Tavern
4. Country House from Võide Village
5. Wooden Church from Sutlepa
6. The Village Swing
7. Jüri-Jaagu Farmstead
8. Kuie Schoolhouse
9. Village Fire Station from Orgmetsa
10. Kalma Windmill

1 Sassi-Jaani Farmstead

A typical north-Estonian farmstead with buildings grouped around a pole-operated well. Grain was kept in the attic and dried by smoke from the family stove.

2 The Köstriaseme Farmstead

The well-preserved interior of this 19th-century farmstead features a weaving loom with the brightly striped bed-spreads *(below)* that would have been produced on it.

3 Kolu Kõrts Tavern

This wood-panelled chamber *(above)* is filled with benches and food is served from a hatch. The stables are now used as an exhibition space.

4 Country House from Võide Village

This wooden house is a wonderful example of the country houses that can still be seen in rural Estonia today, with a perfect 1930s interior.

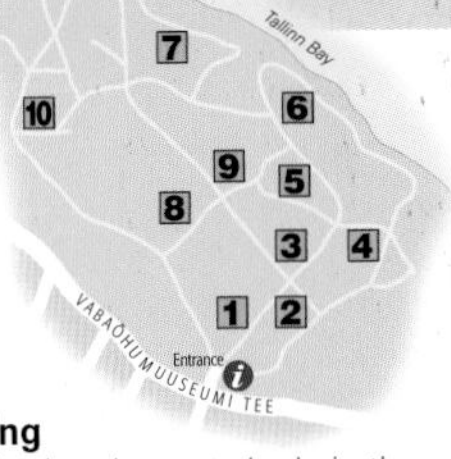

5 Wooden Church from Sutlepa

Originally located in the village of Sutlepa in north-western Estonia, this timber-built church *(right)* rests beneath a thatched roof. A wood-carved pulpit and a cluster of tapering pillars add charm to the interior.

6 The Village Swing

Swings traditionally played a central role in the social life of the Estonian village. It was here that the local youth congregated on summer evenings to play music and swing back and forth singing folk songs.

7 Jüri-Jaagu Farmstead

Representing the island of Muhu, this farmstead showcases the dry-stone-wall construction techniques typical of Estonia's islands *(above)*.

8 Kuie Schoolhouse

The Kuie village schoolhouse provided classrooms as well as living space for the teachers, with a kitchen and parlour in the schoolmistress's wing of the building.

9 Village Fire Station from Orgmetsa

Dating from 1928, this maroon-coloured building with a wooden-shingled roof *(right)* contains a small collection of antiquated horse-drawn fire carts.

10 Kalma Windmill

This large Dutch-style windmill *(below)* has four sails and an intricate wooden-cog mechanism inside.

The Estonian Barn-Dwelling

The typical Estonian farmhouse is the so-called barn-dwelling, a log-built oblong structure comprising living quarters, a threshing room and possibly a cow barn on a single floor. Due to the damp nature of the Estonian climate, grain was stored in the rafters to be dried with the heat and smoke rising from the family stove.

Left **Peter the Great** Centre **Declaration of Independence, 1918** Right **Seal of Valdemar II**

TOP 10 Moments in History

1 1219: Tallinn is Founded by the Danes

Although an Estonian trading post existed here beforehand, the urban history of Tallinn really began in 1219 with the arrival of Danish King Valdemar II. The militant Christian used Tallinn as his base for the conquest of the rest of the country.

2 1345: Tallinn is Sold to the Livonian Order

Denmark's empire-building activities proved too expensive for the crown to bear, and its Estonian possessions were sold to the Livonian Order of German knights. Together with the rest of Estonia, Tallinn became subject to a German-speaking aristocracy.

3 1561: Tallinn Passes to Sweden

The Livonian Order eventually crumbled under pressure from neighbouring powers and Tallinn was absorbed by Sweden. This period was remembered as the "Good Swedish Times" by the locals due to improvements in the legal system and wider provisions for education.

4 1710: Peter the Great Takes Tallinn

Russia and Sweden fought for control over the Baltic region for almost two centuries, a struggle that the Russians, under Peter the Great, finally won in 1710. Tallinn then became a major port city of the Russian Empire.

5 1918: Estonia Becomes an Independent Republic

The Russian Empire collapsed at the end of World War I and Estonia's independence was declared in Tallinn on 24 February 1918. The new country spent several years fighting off invading Bolsheviks and German Freikorps before securing its freedom.

6 1939: The Molotov-Ribbentrop Pact

The end of Estonian independence was signalled in August 1939, when Soviet foreign minister Molotov and his German counterpart Ribbentrop agreed to slice up Eastern Europe between them. Estonia fell within the Soviet half – and was occupied by the Kremlin's troops in June 1940.

Signing of the Molotov-Ribbentrop Pact

7 1945: Re-occupation by the Soviet Union

Nazi Germany declared war on the Soviet Union in June 1941, but after initial defeats the Soviets had re-established

Preceding pages **Epping Tower, The City Walls**

control over Estonia by 1945. Thousands of Estonians were deported to Siberia in 1949 in order to stifle any anti-Soviet opposition.

Demonstrators of the Singing Revolution

8 1988: The Singing Revolution

The loosening of censorship in the late 1980s allowed citizens to openly discuss the injustices they had suffered during Soviet occupation. The country's folk festivals became an important arena for public protest, earning the freedom movement the title of "Singing Revolution".

9 1991: Estonia Regains Independence

The power of the Kremlin was fatally weakened by the unsuccessful Moscow coup of August 1991. The Estonians took full advantage of the power vacuum in the Soviet Union by declaring their independence on 20 August.

10 2004: Estonia Joins the European Union

Estonia was quick to introduce economic reforms in the 1990s and embraced technologies such as the internet with a speed that far outstripped its East-European neighbours. It finally became a part of the European Union in May 2004.

Top 10 Great Estonians

1 Kalevipoeg
Legendary Kalevipoeg (Son of Kalev) is the warrior who is the subject of Estonia's epic poem of the same name.

2 F R Kreutzwald (1803–82)
Provincial doctor who prepared the *Kalevipoeg* stories for publication, giving Estonians their first native-language patriotic text.

3 Carl Robert Jakobson (1841–82)
Founder of the native-language newspaper *Sakala*, which campaigned against the power of German landowners.

4 Lydia Koidula (1843–86)
Lyrical poet whose patriotic poem *Mu Isamaa* (My Fatherland) has been a rallying cry for generations.

5 General Johan Laidoner (1884–1953)
Leader of Estonian forces during the War of Independence, Laidoner defeated Bolshevik and German armies.

6 Konstantin Päts (1874–1956)
Estonia's first independent prime minister, Päts was Head of State throughout the 1930s.

7 Lennart Meri (1929–2006)
Son of Estonians exiled to Siberia, Meri was the president of Estonia from 1992–2000.

8 Jaan Kross (1920–2007)
A writer of historical novels, Kross was a standard bearer for Estonian culture during the Soviet period.

9 Arvo Pärt (b.1935)
Composer of symphonic and choral pieces, Pärt is a pioneer of minimalist music.

10 Carmen Kass (b.1978)
Tallinn-born supermodel who paved the way for other Baltic catwalk stars.

Left **City Museum** Centre **Estonian History Museum** Right **Museum of Applied Art and Design**

Top 10 Museums and Galleries

Entrance, Adamson-Eric Museum

1 Adamson-Eric Museum

Estonia's most versatile 20th-century artist, Adamson-Eric brought his talents to bear on a wide range of disciplines, be it planning the interiors of cafés or painting Estonian rural subjects in traditional oil-on-canvas style *(see p80)*.

2 City Museum

This museum relates the history of the city, and the artifacts here reveal the wealth of medieval Tallinn's mercantile elite. The City Museum is housed in a tall late-Gothic merchant's house – an attraction in itself *(see pp14–15)*.

3 Museum of Occupations

This account of Estonia's occupation by Nazi and Soviet regimes packs a powerful emotional punch. Many of the objects associated with this traumatic period in Estonian history (such as the suitcases belonging to those transported to Siberia) are piled on the floor of the museum for added poignancy *(see pp20–21)*.

4 KUMU Art Museum

Occupying a contemporary building, the national collection of modern art reveals just how varied 20th-century Estonian culture actually was. Even 45 years of Soviet occupation were unable to silence the local avant-garde *(see pp26–9)*.

5 Kadriorg Art Museum

Housed in a palace built for Peter the Great, the opulent interiors of the Kadriorg Art Museum reveal the expensive tastes of Russia's Tsars. A Europe-wide collection of old masters includes artists such as Pieter Brueghel the Younger and Angelika Kauffmann *(see pp24–5)*.

Interior, Kadriorg Art Museum

6 Museum of Applied Art and Design

This historical survey of Estonian applied art showcases the folk-influenced textiles of the 1930s, the pop art-inspired furnishings of the 1960s and the Nordic-flavoured product design of today *(see p80)*.

7 Estonian History Museum

From independence to occupation to independence regained, the 20th century was a turbulent but triumphant experience for the Estonian people. Making use of photos and film clips, this museum is the place to get to grips with Estonia's story *(see p98)*.

8 Air Harbour Maritime Museum

Erected to house the Russian Navy's flying boats in 1916, this cavernous concrete hangar provides the dramatic setting for a maritime history display. The star exhibit is Lembit, a submarine built for the Estonian fleet in 1937 *(see p97)*.

9 Patarei Prison Museum

Another legacy of the Tsarist Empire, this seafront barrack building was used as a prison by both independent Estonia and the Soviet Union. Left untouched since its closure in 2004, the prison is an eerie and unsettling place to visit *(see p97)*.

Museum of Applied Art and Design

10 The Estonian Open-Air Museum

Displaying a huge collection of timber buildings spread over a large park-like area, this is the ideal introduction to Estonian rural life through the ages. Many of the buildings contain original furnishings and handmade textiles, providing a visual feast of Estonian folk art *(see pp30–31)*.

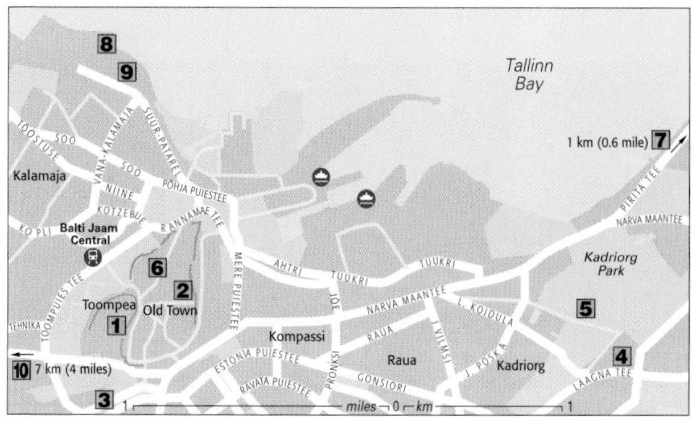

Left **Portrait of the Artist's Mother** Centre **Two Nudes** Right **Estonian Woman**

Top 10 Artworks

1 Red Horses I and II

Estonian artists of the 1970s escaped from Soviet ideology in a number of ways. The bright colours and optimistic outlook of pop art was one such release – Malle Leis's (b.1940) *Red Horses* celebrates natural beauty rather than the greyness of state socialism. *KUMU • Map C5*

A Lady with Child

2 Baroque Pulpit, Dome Church

Local craftsman Christian Ackermann was a master of the baroque style. His furnishings for Tallinn's Dome Church feature swirling columns and richly decorative details *(see pp18–19)*.

3 A Lady with Child

Arnold Akberg (1894–1984) was the most uncompromising of the avant-garde artists who were active in Estonia during the inter-war years. He blended Russian constructivism and French cubism to produce a striking series of revolutionary images. *KUMU • Map C5*

4 Estonian Woman

Tõnu Virve (b.1946) embraced the ambiguity of contemporary western art with this enigmatic painting, leaving the viewer to decide whether it is a celebration of Estonian values or an ironic comment on them. *KUMU • Map C5*

5 Danse Macabre

Some of northern Europe's greatest artists worked in Tallinn during the late Middle Ages, lured by the handsome fees paid by the city's churches. The greatest among them was Bremen's Bernt Notke (c.1435–1508),

Danse Macabre

Lake Villajärv

whose mischievously morbid *Danse Macabre* still spells out a profoundly moral message.
Niguliste Church • Map J4

6 Portrait of the Artist's Mother

Educated at the Imperial Academy of Arts in St Petersburg, Johann Köler (1826–99) was one of the first Estonians to receive a formal art training. He went on to become one of the most accomplished portraitists of the age. *KUMU • Map C5*

7 Two Nudes

Estonia's most accomplished figurative painter of the inter-war years, Adamson-Eric (1902–68) introduced a frisson of eroticism into traditional images of the Estonian peasantry. *Adamson-Eric Museum • Map H4*

8 Pegasus

Made in 1964, this three-pronged piece of aluminium by Edgar Viies (1931–2006) was thought to be the first piece of abstract art in Soviet Estonia, and as such served as a powerful symbol of the changing times. It was originally placed in the Pegasus artists' café, now known as the Fish & Wine restaurant *(see p83)*, where a replica currently stands.
KUMU • Map C5

9 Lake Villajärv

Konrad Mägi (1878–1925) introduced the bright colours and bold brushwork of expressionism into Estonian art, harnessing new techniques to depict the Estonian countryside with a vigour and verve that had never been seen before.
KUMU • Map C5

10 Rusalka Memorial

Erected in 1902 to honour the dead of the Rusalka (a Russian warship that sunk in the Baltic Sea in September 1893), this elegant bronze statue of an angel was produced by Amandus Adamson (1855–1929), Estonia's first academically trained sculptor. *Kadriorg Park • Map C4*

Rusalka Memorial

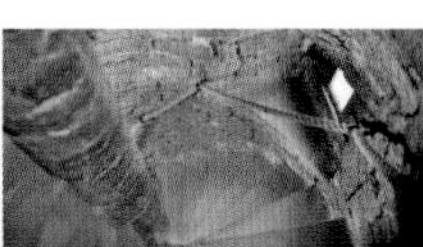

Left **Pirita Convent ruins** Centre **Spiral staircase, Dome Church** Right **St Simeon's Church**

Top 10 Churches

1 Dome Church (Cathedral of St Mary the Virgin)

More spacious on the inside than it initially appears on the outside, Tallinn's Lutheran cathedral contains several funerary monuments from throughout the ages, as well as a riot of baroque woodcarving *(see pp18–19)*.

2 Church of the Holy Ghost

A pencil-thin belfry and an attractive medieval clock add charm to the whitewashed exterior of this dainty church. Inside, an imposing altarpiece by Bernt Notke provides a focus for visitors' awe *(see p9)*.

3 Orthodox Cathedral of Alexander Nevsky

With an array of domes and towers, this 19th-century church represents Orthodox Tallinn at its most flamboyant. It is dedicated to Alexander Nevsky, the 13th-century Prince of Novgorod, who repelled German invaders and became a symbol of Russian military prowess *(see p69)*.

4 Niguliste Church

A fortified church whose tower was built to withstand attacks by Tallinn's enemies, the Niguliste (St Nicholas's) is home to a spectacular collection of medieval artworks, none more riveting than Bernt Notke's *Danse Macabre (see pp12–13)*.

5 Oleviste Church

The slender steeple of 14th-century Oleviste (St Olaf's) Church was the skyscraper of its day, and still dwarfs the surrounding buildings of Tallinn's Old Town *(see p10)*.

6 St John's Church

A fine example of the 19th-century craze for medieval styles, this church contains a

Orthodox Cathedral of Alexander Nevsky

neogothic altarpiece and pulpit. It is the main city-centre place of worship for Tallinn's Lutheran population. Ⓢ *Map J4*

7 Church of St Simeon and the Prophetess Hanna

One of the few surviving timber churches in central Tallinn, this church was relegated to the role of basketball court during the Soviet period and has only recently been restored. Inside lies a glittering collection of orthodox icons *(see p90)*.

8 Pirita Convent

The centrepiece of a thriving Brigittine monastery in the 15th century, the high-gabled Pirita Convent was burned by marauding Russians in the 1550s. It survived as a roofless shell to become modern-day Tallinn's most haunting ruin *(see p98)*.

9 St Nicholas's Orthodox Church

To experience the intimate spiritual atmosphere of a typical Orthodox church, head for busy little St Nicholas's in the Old Town. The flickering of candles,

Church of St Simeon & the Prophetess Hanna

sparkle of gilded icons and fragrance of incense will leave an impression *(see p80)*.

10 Wooden Church from Sutlepa

The green meadows of the Estonian Open-Air Museum provide the setting for this typical example of rural wooden architecture, hailing from the Swede-inhabited village of Sutlepa on Estonia's northwestern coast *(see p31)*.

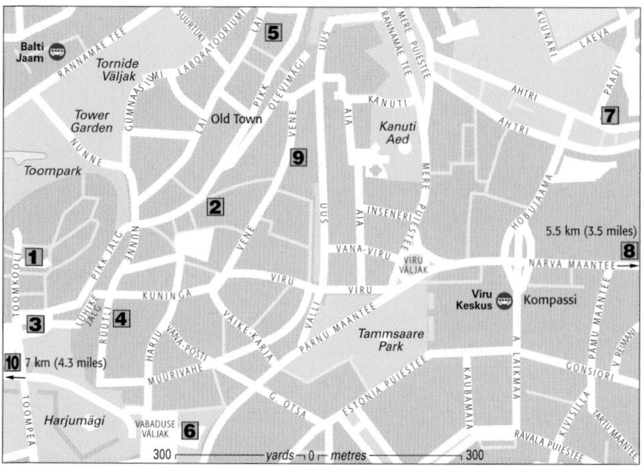

Left **Wine cellar, Stenhus** Right **Fish & Wine restaurant**

Top 10 Restaurants

1 Chedi

Chic decor and Asian-Estonian culinary fusion combine to produce one of Tallinn's most stylish dining experiences. The menu of this fine dining restaurant includes something for everyone, although it is the exotically spiced fish options that set the mouth watering *(see p83)*.

2 Ö

When it comes to Estonian-European fusion, Ö leads the way with locally-sourced pork, fish, and fowl dishes presented in a style that wouldn't look out of place in the best French restaurants. Boasting one of Tallinn's coolest contemporary-design interiors, this is a hipster's hangout and gourmet destination rolled into one *(see p93)*.

3 Olde Hansa

Longest established of Tallinn's medieval themed restaurants, Olde Hansa, located in central Tallinn, is nowadays something of an institution. It still scores top marks when it comes to historical ambience, hearty food and enjoyable theatricality – with wait-staff and minstrels greeting the guests *(see p82)*.

Street sign, Olde Hansa

4 Museum

Located in a former fire station, Museum belies its name with contemporary lounge-bar furnishings and a cosmopolitan menu. Sushi and Mediterranean salads are among the dishes on offer. It is run by the same team that operates Chedi and Ö *(see p83)*.

Interior, Museum restaurant

5 Kohvik Moon

An imaginative mixture of Estonian and modern-European food sets the tone in this café-restaurant, located in the up-and-coming Kalamaja district. Moon means "poppy" in Estonian, and the flower features as a recurring design motif in the cool, contemporary interior *(see p93)*.

6 Balthasar

Housed in a medieval building that exudes historical atmosphere, Balthasar has long been one of Tallinn's destination restaurants. Garlic is the trademark ingredient, although the range of north-European meat and fish dishes allows plenty of choice *(see p82)*.

7 Fish & Wine

Quality Mediterranean seafood and a good wine list is the order of the day in this swanky restaurant on three levels. Fish & Wine is housed in the marvellously modernist Pegasus building, a landmark of Estonian architecture that originally served as an artists' café in the 1960s *(see p83)*.

8 Ribe

The refined and relaxing Ribe is a leading exponent of modern Estonian cuisine. It takes the north-European culinary repertoire of meat, fish and game, and presents it in a contemporary and stylish way. The decor is soothing *(see p82)*.

9 Stenhus

Exquisite food, exemplary service and a beautifully restored 13th-century cellar have made Stenhus one of Tallinn's outstanding culinary addresses. Duck, fresh fish and lamb figure prominently in the French-Estonian menu's classic mains *(see p82)*.

Entrance, Balthasar

10 Von Krahli Aed

For fine food in an informal environment there are few better places than Von Krahli Aed, attached to the theatre and bar of the same name. Estonian, Mediterranean and vegetarian options jostle for attention on the restaurant's inventive and varied menu *(see p82)*.

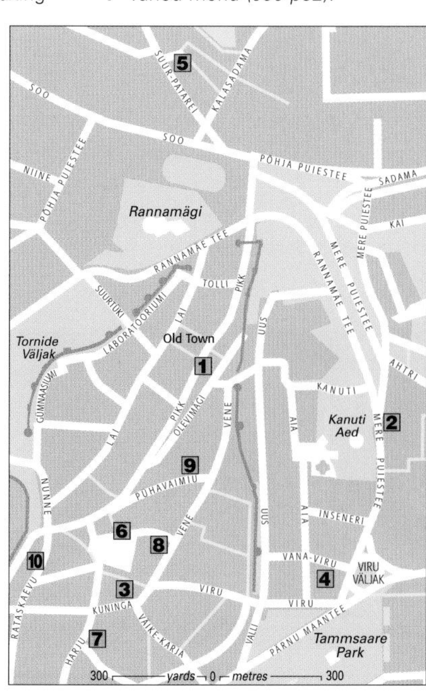

Left **NUKU Puppet Museum** Centre **AHHAA Science Centre** Right **Toomas the Train**

Top 10 Children's Attractions

1 Tallinn Zoo

Occupying a spacious, partly wooded site west of the town centre, Tallinn Zoo is easy to combine with a visit to the nearby Estonian Open-Air Museum *(see pp30–31)*. The zoo's highlights include the elephant house, European bison enclosure and Amur leopards – the latter are among the world's rarest cats *(see p100)*.

2 Estonian State Puppet and Youth Theatre (NUKU)

A highly respected institution offering a year-round repertoire of puppet theatre and live action shows for children. Performances are in Estonian but puppet-led storytelling can be spellbinding, whatever the language. Shows usually start at noon. *Lai 1 • Map H3 • www.nuku.ee*

3 AHHAA Science Centre

This hands-on discovery centre planned by Tartu University's science department aims to make science more interesting for young teenagers. The centre's changing exhibits and 4D cinema have an interactive nature and focus on social issues such as health *(see p92)*.

Tallinn Zoo

4 Children's Play Park

Tallinn's biggest children's play park offers a traditional menu of climbing frames, carousels, sandpits and slides. It is right in the middle of Kadriorg Park, making it the perfect centrepiece of a family outing *(see pp22–3)*.

Children's Play Park

5 Energy Discovery Centre

This former power station houses endless halls of strange-looking power-generating machines, designed to show the science that lies behind our daily energy needs. The exhibits are interactive but instructions are frequently in Estonian only *(see p92)*.

6 Miia-Milla Manda

Occupying a colonnaded pavilion next to the Kadriorg Play Park, Miia-Milla Manda aims to entertain younger children with a variety of educative play situations such as posting toys from a post office and spelling out words with huge alphabet letters. *Koidula 21c • Map C5 • 601 7057 • Open noon–6pm Tue–Sun • Tram 1, 3 • www.linnamuuseum.ee/miiamillamanda*

7 NUKU Puppet Museum

Drawing on the 50-year history of the NUKU Theatre, this museum presents inventively designed puppets throughout the ages. The archly amusing "Chamber of Horrors" will have visitors groaning with fake terror *(see p78)*.

8 Tallinn Skypark

Tallinn Skypark has a large trampoline court featuring 14 floor and nine wall trampolines. A play area with toboggan slides makes this the perfect place to let off steam after a day's sightseeing. *Pärnu mnt. 139E • Map A6 • 656 8400 • Open noon–10pm Mon–Fri, 10am–10pm Sat & Sun • Bus 18 from Viru Keskus Bus Terminal • www.skypark.ee*

Children playing at the Tallinn Skypark

9 Toomas the Train

Departing from Kullassepa just off the main Town Hall Square, Toomas takes you on a 20-minute tour of the Old Town. *Map J3 • Open noon–5pm: daily Jun–Aug; weekends May & Sept • Adm (free with Tallinn card)*

10 Play Park, Estonian Open-Air Museum

Located just outside Kolu Kõrts tavern *(see p101)*, all the swings and roundabouts in this park are handmade from wood by craftsmen. The museum also contains traditional Estonian swings: huge platforms made for several people to stand on at once. *Map A1*

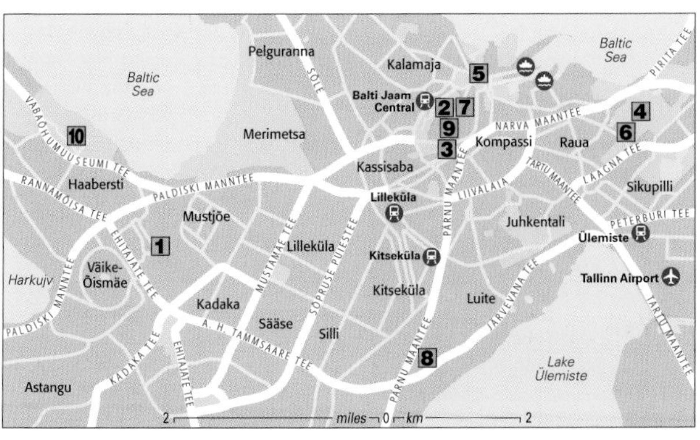

Left **Pork knuckle with sauerkraut** Centre **Smoked eel** Right **Red caviar on rye bread**

TOP 10 Culinary Specialities

1 Rye Bread

Dark brown rye bread *(leib)* has been the staple food of Estonia for centuries and is served with every meal of the day. High in fibre and minerals and relatively low in fat, it is an ultra-healthy addition to your holiday diet.

2 Mannapuder

The Estonian diet is full of porridges and none is more popular than *mannapuder* (semolina porridge), which is eaten either for breakfast or as a dessert later in the day. It is frequently served with a dollop of jam or *kissell* (a jelly-like fruit preserve).

3 Verivorst

Verivorst is a favourite pork product – a blood sausage made from pig's blood and barley meal. As with other Estonian meat dishes, sauerkraut is the ideal accompaniment.

Verivorst, a type of blood sausage

4 Rosolje

Salads in Estonia usually feature pickled vegetables and local dairy products and *rosolje* is no exception. The main ingredients are beetroot, potato, egg and cream – the beetroot produces a distinctive pink colour. Salted herring usually features in the *rosolje* mix, although recipes differ from one establishment to the next.

Hernesupp

5 Hernesupp

Customarily served with a generous garnish of crispy bacon fat and fried onions, *hernesupp* (split-pea soup) is a traditional peasant lunchtime dish that nowadays frequently features as the standard side-order when quaffing several rounds of beer.

6 Karbonaad

The most common main course on any Estonian menu is the *karbonaad*, a pork cutlet coated in rich batter. It is almost invariably served with *hapukapsad* (sauerkraut) or *mulgikapsad* (a potato, sauerkraut and onion mix).

7 Pirukas

The *pirukas* is a small crescent shaped pie made from bready dough, and filled with a variety of savoury items – usually cabbage, mushroom or bacon bits. Most Estonian cafés display a selection of *pirukas* on the counter and they're excellent as a quick daytime snack.

8 Mulgipuder

A fry-up of mashed potato, barley porridge, pork fat and onion, *mulgipuder* makes a great accompaniment to a traditional Estonian meat dish. It is also a winter-warming stomach filler in its own right.

9 Smoked Eel

Smoked eel is a highly regarded delicacy, and it features on many restaurant and café menus as a starter or tasty little snack.

10 Herring

Whether salted, pickled or smoked, the Baltic herring *(räim)* occupies a central place in the Estonian national diet. It is usually served as an ingredient in salads or on its own as a starter. Note that a plate of salted herring also makes the ideal accompaniment to a round of evening vodkas.

Tinned herring

Top 10 Estonian Drinks

1 Vana Tallinn

A bottle of this syrupy amber-coloured liqueur is the archetypal Tallinn souvenir.

2 Liivimaa Palsam

A dark-brown, mildly bitter spirit made from herbs, this is the ideal stomach settler.

3 Hõõgvein

This spicy mulled wine serves as the great winter warmer.

4 Kali

A fermented rye-bread drink similar to the Russian *kvass*, kali is a refreshing alternative to international soft-drink brands and is rich in Vitamin B.

5 Põltsamaa Wine

Sweet fruity wine made from summer berries. All the fresh produce used in Põltsamaa wine is grown in Estonia.

6 Vodka

Still the most popular spirit – Viru Valge is the main brand.

7 Kama

A paste made from oat, barley and wheat flour, mixed with milk or *kefir* to make a refreshing breakfast drink.

8 Lager Beer

The country's staple tipple, churned out by the tanker load by big brewers Saku and A Le Coq.

9 Saaremaa X

Strong, flavoursome dark beer brewed on the island of Saaremaa.

10 Soviet-style Champagne

Enjoyable, cheap and fruity, sparkling wine from Russia and the Ukraine is still a common feature in Estonian supermarkets.

Left **Drink Bar & Grill** Right **Café VS**

TOP 10 Pubs and Bars

1 Café VS

The post-industrial decor and sleek metallic surfaces make this an unlikely place to settle down with a pint and a curry, but it's precisely this mixture of homely bar food and futuristic design features that makes Café VS so enduringly popular. DJ-driven music in the evenings provides extra appeal to sticking around *(see p93)*.

2 Lounge 24

Offering fantastic views of the Tallinn skyline from its location on the 24th floor of the Radisson Blu hotel, Lounge 24 is one of the few bars outside the Old Town that demand to be treated as a destination. Stylish cocktails, a tasty menu of light meals and a trendy decor complete the experience *(see p93)*.

3 Musi

A popular well-stocked wine bar that succeeds in being slightly different, Musi consists of a front room with old-fashioned furniture and lacy tablecloths, and a lounge-style back room decked out in modern, pop art bright colours *(see p86)*. It is located right opposite Niguliste Church *(see pp12–13)*.

4 Karja Kelder

An early 20th-century beer hall which has retained its wooden fittings and stained glass, the "Beer Cellar" draws all ages and all types with its unbeatably traditional pub atmosphere. There's an extensive selection of imported beers on offer and the food is good value for money *(see p87)*.

Panoramic view of Tallinn from Lounge 24

Hell Hunt pub

5 Osteria del Gallo Nero

A welcoming aroma of cured hams and pungent cheese hits you as you cross the threshold of this cosy Italian delicatessen-cum-wine bar. Checked tablecloths and wooden furnishings add to the friendly, relaxed ambience *(see p86)*.

6 Hell Hunt

This long established favourite of Tallinn's expat community just never goes out of fashion, yet hasn't been spoiled by its place on the tourist route. Try Hell Hunt's own-brand beer: it is excellent and comes in both light and porter versions *(see p87)*.

7 Deja Vu

Dance the night away to funky DJ sets and regular live music at this stylish bar. When you need a break from the party, head upstairs and enjoy a sumptuous cocktail or a hookah pipe while relaxing on a sofa in the comfortable lounge area. The kitchen serves tasty snacks and meals late into the night *(see p86)*.

8 Drink Bar & Grill

With a lack of in-your-face design touches, absence of loud music and a profusion of fine ales, this bar is the nearest central Tallinn comes to a friendly neighbourhood pub. The Drink Bar & Grill offers a good choice of international beers on tap and plenty more in bottles *(see p87)*.

9 Embassy Lounge

A bare, concrete space furnished with comfy sofas and designer accessories, the Embassy is a cool combination of the rough and the smooth. An extensive menu of shots and cocktails provides ample reason to stick around *(see p86)*.

10 Valli Baar

Probably the only place in the Old Town that has the feel of a local bar full of earnestly quaffing locals, Valli Baar is the perfect antidote to raucous disco-pubs and dressed-up cocktail lounges *(see p87)*.

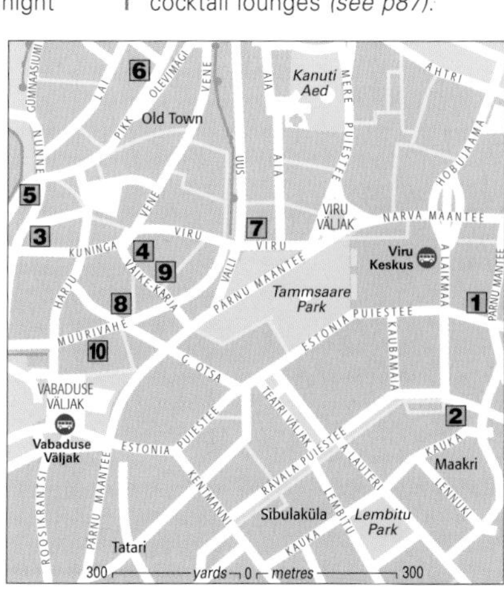

Left **Kehrwieder** Centre **Komeet, Solaris Mall** Right **Matilda Café**

TOP 10 Cafés

1 Kehrwieder
Despite being right on the tourist-thronged main square, Kehrwieder retains a certain individuality. The coffee is strong and the cheesecakes are outstanding *(see p85)*.

2 Komeet
Located on the top floor of Solaris *(see p59)*, Komeet's roof garden is the perfect place to relax and watch the sun slowly sinking behind the Old Town's spires *(see p93)*.

3 Kõrts Inn Krug
Located within the bowels of Tallinn's medieval Town Hall, this café mixes modern day coffee-shop convenience with plenty in the way of Estonian tradition. The excellent range of savoury *pirukas* are well worth nibbling your way through *(see p85)*.

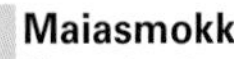

4 Maiasmokk
Since its foundation in the mid-19th century Maiasmokk has become something of a Tallinn institution, serving up coffee, pastries, cakes and marzipan in charmingly old-fashioned, wood-panelled rooms *(see p11)*.

Maiasmokk café

5 Matilda
A cosy café in the crook of Lühike jalg, the alleyway that wends its way up towards Toompea hill, Matilda is highly regarded for its cakes, cheese-cakes and meringues *(see p85)*.

6 Chocolaterie Pierre
With tables strewn across a cobbled alley bordered by craft workshops, there are few better locations for coffee and cake than this. The delicious handmade chocolates must be tasted *(see p85)*.

Chocolaterie Pierre

7 Spirit Café
A varied and interesting international menu and

daily lunchtime specials make Spirit a great spot for a midday break *(see p93)*.

8 Anneli Viik
Handmade truffles and chocolates are the stars of the show at this small, smart café. You can watch the chocolate-makers at work behind a glass partition and purchase boxed selections to take away *(see p85)*.

9 NOP Café
An old wooden house in a suburban street is the setting for this supremely relaxing café and food shop that excels in delicious vegetarian dishes. Bright decor and a children's play area help sustain the happy mood *(see p101)*.

10 Bogapott
The ideal spot for taking a breather while strolling around Toompea, Bogapott serves up tea and coffee in the quirky mugs made in the ceramics studio next door. Take a break in its plant-filled courtyard or the high-ceilinged, medieval interior of this family-run café *(see p73)*.

Entrance, Bogapott café

Top 10 Sweet Treats

1 Pancakes
Filled with jam or seasonal fruits, pancakes are a standard inclusion on café menus.

2 Marzipan
This almond and sugar paste features heavily in the confections produced by Tallinn's traditional cafés.

3 Chocolate Truffles
Several cafés specialize in the production of these delicious handmade sweets.

4 Karask
A sweet bread containing barley and carrot, available at traditional bakeries.

5 Napoleonikook
Named after Napoleon, this custard-filled French pastry is enormously popular in Estonia.

6 Carrot Cake
The carrot is something of a national vegetable in Estonia. Numerous delicious variations of carrot cake *(porgandikook)* abound in its bakeries.

7 Cheesecake
Another international favourite adopted by the Estonians, cheesecake *(kohupiimakook)* frequently comes covered in seasonal berries or fruits.

8 Kissell
A sweet soup made from cranberries, redcurrents or other summer fruits, *kissell* can be drunk on its own or combined with porridge.

9 Bubert
A smooth semolina pudding enriched with egg and garnished with fruit.

10 Mulgikorp
A Danish pastry filled with sweetened cheese, *mulgikorp* is a staple of cafés and bakeries throughout the city.

Left **Birgitta Festival** Right **Tallinn Medieval Days**

Festivals and Events

1 Light Festival

Held in January when the dark Baltic nights are at their longest, Tallinn's Light Festival *(Valgusfestival)* involves a programme of open-air light installations and fire sculptures set against the backdrop of the Old Town. *www.valgusfestival.ee*

2 Shrovetide

February is Shrovetide *(Vastlapaev)* time in Estonia and is marked by downhill sledge racing and a pre-Lenten feast of pigs' trotters and pea soup. Tallinn's Open-Air Museum *(see pp30–31)* organizes a full day of Shrove Tuesday events and you will find all kinds of impromptu Shrovetide fun taking place throughout the city. *www.evm.ee*

3 Jazzkaar

Even in Soviet times Tallinn was known for its cutting-edge jazz – a tradition continued by the Jazzkaar festival, which brings international artists to Tallinn every April. Performances take place throughout the city, frequently in intimate gallery and museum spaces. *www.jazzkaar.ee*

4 Tallinn Old Town Days

One of the most accessible events for visitors, Tallinn Old Town Days *(Tallinna Vanalinna Päevad)* takes place in early June. Free concerts are held on the Town Hall Square, while the Old Town is taken over by a succession of enjoyably bizarre events. *www.vanalinnapaevad.ee*

5 Midsummer's Night

Also known as St John's Eve *(Jaanipaev)*, this is a very important event for Estonians, who celebrate by drinking and carousing all night with friends.

6 Tallinn Medieval Days

Early July sees this weekend-long celebration of Tallinn's medieval heritage, with costumed parades and knightly jousts entertaining large crowds. Traditional crafts such as iron-mongery, weaving and pottery are also celebrated, with open-air workshops and a multitude of stalls. *www.folkart.ee*

7 Beer Summer

Taking place in mid-July, Beer Summer *(Õllesummer)* is

Beer Summer festival

both the country's biggest beer festival and a major pop-rock event. Live performances lure crowds to the Song Festival Grounds in Kadriorg. ⊗ *www.ollesummer.ee*

A performance during Birgitta Festival

8 Birgitta Festival

Opera and ballet are the focus of this prestigious mid-August event, with performances staged in the evocative ruins of the Brigittine convent in Pirita *(see p98)*. Tickets can be hard to come by so be sure to reserve in advance. ⊗ *www.birgitta.ee*

9 Nargen Music Festival

The Nargen Festival (Aug–Sep) is famous for making use of evocative concert spaces – notably semi-derelict buildings on the island of Naisaar north of Tallinn. Music by contemporary Estonian composers Arvo Pärt and Veljo Tormis plays a major role in the festival. ⊗ *www.nargenfestival.ee*

10 Advent Market

A great place to pick up handicrafts, local foodstuffs and folk items, Advent Market runs from early December until January 7th. Copious quantities of *Hõõgvein* (hot mulled wine) help to make up for the sub-zero temperatures. ⊗ *Map J3*

Top 10 National Commemoration Days

1 2 February: Tartu Peace Treaty Day
A reference to the 1920 treaty that ended hostilities between Estonia and the Soviet Union.

2 24 February: Independence Day
This date marks the declaration of independence made in 1918, ending three centuries of subjugation to the Tsarist Empire.

3 14 March: Native Language Day
Celebration of Estonian culture on the birthday of poet Kristjan Jaak Peterson (1801–22).

4 4 June: National Flag Day
The Estonian flag was ceremonially adopted in Otepää village on this day in 1884.

5 14 June: Commemoration Day
In honour of those who were deported to the Soviet east in 1941 and 1949.

6 23 June: Victory Day
The anniversary of the Estonian army's victory over the Iron Division of German General von der Goltz in the Battle of Cesis (1919).

7 20 August: Restoration of Independence Day
This national holiday marks the restoration of Estonian independence in 1991.

8 23 August: Remembrance Day
Dedicated to the victims of both Fascism and Communism.

9 22 September: Resistance Day
Commemorating Otto Tief's attempt to restore Estonian independence in 1944.

10 16 November: Sovereignty Day
Marking the Estonian Supreme Soviet's Declaration of Sovereignty in 1989.

Left **Eesti kasitöö** Centre **Rotermann Quarter mall** Right **Komeet café, Solaris**

TOP 10 Places to Shop

1 Katariina Gild

For traditional crafts made by skilled craftspeople, Katariina Gild is the best place – a series of artisans' workshops lining a pedestrian alley. Ceramics, ironmongery, textile weaving, millinery and quilt making are all represented, making this an ideal spot to purchase high quality, handmade souvenirs. *Katariina käik • Map K3 • Open noon–6pm Mon–Sat • www.katariinagild.eu*

2 Masters' Courtyard

Located in the alleyway running parallel to Katariina Gild, the Masters' Courtyard *(Meistrite hoov)* also features ceramics and ironmongery workshops but with a quirky artistic flavour. The handmade chocolates on offer at Chocolaterie Pierre *(see p52)* are an added bonus. *Vene 6 • Map J3 • Open 10am–6pm • www.hoov.ee*

3 Müürivahe

An alleyway running beneath Tallinn's medieval walls, Müürivahe is famous for its traditional jumpers, socks, hats and mittens, sold at open stalls by local knitters. *Map K3 • Open 9am–5pm*

Display at shop entrance, Müürivahe

4 Rotermann Quarter

In addition to being an upmarket mall, Rotermann Quarter is also the site of the Kalev Candy Shop. Visitors can create and decorate their own handmade Marzipan figurines and fine chocolates in the shop's Master's Chamber. During summer, there is an organic food market in the pedestrian plaza outside. *Rotermann Rosini 7 • Map L3 • Open 10am–8pm Mon–Sat, 11am–6pm Sun • www.kalev.ee*

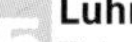

5 Lühike jalg

This alleyway leading up towards Castle Hill is home to Tallinn's quirkiest souvenir shops, with ceramics, textiles and jewellery available from a trio of specialist outlets. *Map H4*

Masters' Courtyard

6 Eesti kasitöö

Located in the centre of the Old Town, Eesti kasitöö (Estonian Handicraft) is the oldest and most reliable outlet for handmade felt hats, linen shirts, folk-patterned bedspreads

Preceding pages **Clock atop Church of the Holy Ghost**

and jumpers – many of which are made in studios on the premises *(see p84)*.

7 Solaris Centre

Tallinn boasts a growing number of shopping malls and Solaris is the easiest to navigate, with shops on three floors, varied eating and drinking options, a cinema and a roof-top café *(see p52)*.
Estonia pst 9 • Map K5 • 615 5100 • Open 10am–9pm • www.solaris.ee

8 Fish Market

The fish market takes place every Saturday in the small *Kalasadam* (Fishermen's Harbour) north of the Old Town. This is a great place to pick up fresh fish, marinated seafood and Baltic delicacies such as smoked eel.
Map B4 • Open 10am–4pm Sat

Fish market

9 Jaama Turg

Located to the eastern side of Balti Jaam train station, this maze of kiosks sells everything from fresh fruit to mobile phones. *Kopli 1 • Map G2 • 644 6128 • Open 9am–6pm Mon–Fri, 9am–5pm Sat–Sun*

10 Central Market

A short tram ride from the Old Town, Tallinn's Central Market *(Keskturg)* is the main place for fresh fruit, vegetables and seasonal local produce.
Keldrimäe 9 • Map M6 • 660 6304 • Open 7am–5pm

Top 10 Souvenirs

1 Amber
Jewellery fashioned from this fossilized resin from the Baltic Sea makes the perfect souvenir.

2 Ironmongery
Tallinn is the ideal place to seek out individually crafted items, be it a a door-knocker or a set of garden furniture.

3 Ceramics
Quality pottery is another Tallinn tradition, with everything from one-off vases to practical tableware on offer.

4 Chocolate
Handmade chocolates and truffles are a major feature of the local café scene and make for ideal gifts.

5 Linen
Stylish linen products, from tablecloths to summer dresses, are available from a number of Old Town shops.

6 Marzipan
Marzipan has a centuries-old tradition in Tallinn, with Maiasmokk café *(see p52)* being the spot for handmade marzipan sweets.

7 Spirits
Syrupy-sweet Vana Tallinn liqueur is Tallinn's standout liquid souvenir, although there are plenty other local vodkas to choose from too.

8 Wood
Wooden kitchen utensils and toys make practical and long-lasting souvenirs.

9 Woollens
Tallinn is a great place to buy hand-knitted hats, mittens, socks and sweaters, patterned with Estonian folk motifs.

10 Felt Hats
Highly individual and also highly wearable, Tallinn's hand crafted felt hats give evidence of the city's artistic streak.

Take tram no. 2 or 4 to get to Central Market (Keskturg).

Left **Clazz** Centre **Hollywood** Right **Korter**

Top 10 Nightlife Spots

1 BonBon

Decked out in glam retro fittings, BonBon attracts slightly older, more affluent clubbers, although energy levels remain high on the dance floor. If you want to party with Tallinn's A-list then BonBon is your best bet. *Mere pst 6e • Map L3 • 5400 5411 • Open 11pm–5am Fri & Sat*

2 Hollywood

This multi-level club in a former cinema in the Old Town is great for a hedonistic Friday night out. Very popular with young locals, Hollywood delivers a dance floor filling blend of contemporary pop and retro-disco. *Vana-Posti 8 • Map J4 • Open 11pm onwards Wed–Sat*

3 Privé

Established by Tallinn's cutting-edge DJ crews, this exclusive club attracts the local fashionistas with its themed nights and international disc-spinning guests. Study the posters and find out who's manning the turntables before forking out for the entrance fee. *Harju 6 • Map J4 • 631 0580 • Open midnight–5am Wed–Sat*

4 Korter

A starkly under-decorated post-industrial space hidden away in a courtyard of the Rotermann Quarter, the "Apartment" will suit those who know their dub-step from their drum 'n' bass. International DJs and live acts fill out the programme at this cutting edge place. The drinks are reasonably priced. *Roseni 9 • Map L3 • 509 4339 • Open 11pm–5am Fri & Sat*

Dance floor, Privé

5 Café Amigo

Situated below the Sokos Hotel Viru, Café Amigo attracts a healthy blend of locals and outsiders. This is an enjoyably mainstream, all-ages-welcome dance venue, with frequent live appearances by Estonia's rock-pop aristocracy. *Viru Väljak 4 • Map L4 • 680 9380 • Open 10pm–4am Sun–Thu, 10pm–5am Fri–Sat • www.amigo.ee*

6 Balou

Affordable, friendly and not too flashy, Balou is a basement-bound Old Town haunt that serves up a nightly menu of sharp but accessible house and techno beats. It has garnered a solid local following as a result. *Rüütli 18 • Map H4 • 5370 6082 • Open 11pm–6am Thu–Sat*

7 Clazz

With a three-room interior that looks like an upmarket bar, comfortable pub and cocktail lounge rolled into one, Clazz is a welcoming place to enjoy live jazz and blues. DJs get the floor moving at weekends *(see p86)*.

8 X Baar

A short hop south of the Old Town, X Baar is one of Tallinn's longest-serving gay destinations and strikes the right balance between raucous disco-driven fun and relaxing friendly atmosphere. The dance floor area is augmented by a relaxation room and pool table. *Tatari 1 • Map J5 • 644 0121 • Open 4pm–1am Mon–Thu, 2pm–3am Fri & Sat, 2pm–1am Sun*

Interior, Von Krahl

9 Von Krahl

This laid-back theatre bar becomes a live music and club venue at weekends, when student types and arty people crowd in to enjoy indie bands and alternative DJs *(see p86)*.

10 Venus

Venus pulls in party-happy locals with mainstream disco-pop and frequent fancy-dress nights. Entrance is usually free Sunday–Tuesday, when it's a popular stop on any nocturnal itinerary. *Vana-Viru 14 • Map K3 • 551 9999 • Open 10pm–4am Mon–Thu, 10pm–5am Fri & Sat*

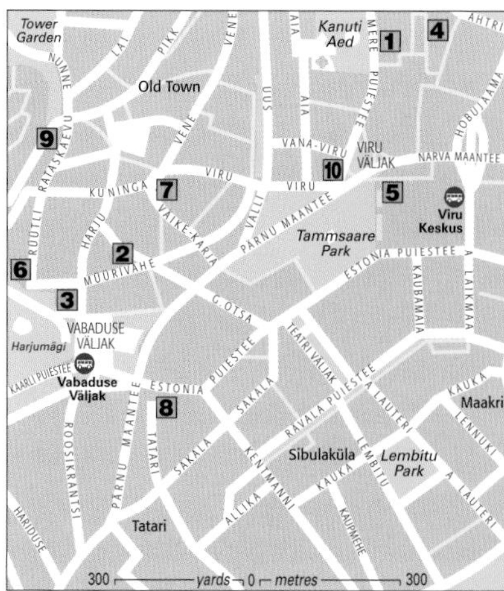

Left **Stroomi beach** Centre **Picnicking at Kadriorg Park** Right **Kalev Water Park**

TOP 10 Ways to Unwind

1 Feeding the Ducks at Snelli Pond

Formed from what's left of Tallinn's former moat, Snelli pond *(Snelli tiik)* now serves as the focus of a city-centre park – popular with waterfowl and humans alike. *Toompark • Map G4*

2 Splashing Around at the Kalev Water Park

Enjoying a location right on the border of the Old Town, this indoor pool is well equipped with water slides, Jacuzzi pools and shallow areas for children. The adjoining spa centre offers all manner of massage and beauty treatments. *Aia 18 • Map K2 • Pool: 649 3370; Spa Centre: 649 3350 • Open 6:45am–9:30pm Mon–Fri; 8am–9:30pm Sat & Sun • Adm • www.kalevspa.ee*

Kalev Water Park

3 Paddling at Pirita Beach

A short bus ride from the centre, this 3-km (2-mile) long crescent of fine white sand backed by pines is perfect for strolling in winter or sunbathing in summer. The western end of the beach is popular with windsurfers, while there is plenty by way of children's play areas further east. *Map D2*

4 Picnicking at Kadriorg Park

Partially shaded by tree cover, the verdant meadows of Kadriorg Park are the perfect place to lay down a picnic blanket. Alternatively head for the Rusalka Memorial just beyond the northeast boundary of the park, where a belt of shoreside dunes backed by trees provides plenty of space in which to sprawl *(see pp22–3)*.

5 Taking a Sauna

A session in the sauna is an essential part of Estonian life, especially in winter when it has a revitalizing effect on weary limbs. Almost every hotel will have an on-site sauna which can be booked by guests – otherwise head for a swimming pool or spa centre such as the Kalev Water Park.

6 Watching a Film at the Solaris Centre

The state-of-the-art Solaris Centre houses two cinemas. The Solaris Kino Multiplex screens popular

Bus nos. 1, 1A, 34 and 38 from Viru Keskus will take you to Pirita beach.

international movies in the original language, while the Artis Cinema showcases art-house films. The variety of restaurants and cafés at the Solaris shopping centre provide plenty of opportunities for pre- or post-show refreshment *(see p59)*. *16 105 • www.solariskino.ee*

Solaris Kino Multiplex, Solaris Centre

7 Sunset at Stroomi Beach

While not as fashionable as the beach at Pirita, the 2-km (1.2-mile) long strand in the suburb of Stroomi comes into its own on spring and summer evenings, when the sun sinks over the wooded coast to the west. *Tram 1 or 2 to Maleva followed by a 10-minute walk through Kopli park*

8 Taking to the Ice on Harju

Visit Tallinn in the winter months and you'll find an outdoor skating rink in the heart of the Old Town. Backed by a picturesque ensemble of historic buildings, the ice rink at Harju is a popular spot for skaters and spectators alike. Skates can be rented on the spot and there is a vibrant café-bar area beside the ice. *Map J4 • Ice rink: 610 1035 • Open 10am–10pm Nov–Mar • Adm*

9 Karting

For an adrenaline-rushing alternative to strolling around Tallinn's historic sights, take to the indoor circuit of the Triobet Kart Centre on the southern outskirts of the city. Book in advance to be sure of a slot. *Pärnu mnt. 558a • 679 8300 • Open 2pm–10pm Mon–Fri, noon–10pm Sat & Sun • www.hobikart.ee*

10 Cycling around the Estonian Open-Air Museum

With woodland, grassy meadows and timber village houses spread over a large area, the Estonian Open-Air Museum is the nearest you can get to a day out in the Estonian countryside without actually leaving the city. An ideal way to tour the site is to pedal around on a bike, which can be rented at the entrance to the museum *(see pp30–31)*.

Cycling, Open-Air Museum

Left **Lahemaa National Park** Centre **Tartu University** Right **Wooden door carving, Pärnu**

TOP 10 Day Trips from Tallinn

1 Aegna Island

Served by daily ferries from May to September, the island of Aegna offers an attractive mixture of rock-strewn coast, sandy beaches and great views back towards the city. *Map B1 • Ferry from the Kalasadama port north of the Old Town; www.veeteed.com*

2 Naissaar

About 10 km (6.2 miles) north of Tallinn, this forested island is dotted with abandoned naval installations dating back to the Tsarist era. Crisscrossed by trails, Naissaar is perfect for leisurely exploration on foot or by bike. *Map A1 • Ferry (weekends only May–Oct) from the Admiralty Basin on the east side of Tallinn's main ferry port; www.monica.ee*

3 Lahemaa National Park

The Estonian countryside is noted for its dense forests, boggy heaths and boulder-strewn coastline, all of which can be admired in the Lahemaa National Park, an hour's drive east from Tallinn. Well-signed nature trails provide access to unspoiled natural wilderness. *Map B1 • Bus from Tallinn bus station • Day trips to the park – cycling or walking tours – are organized by Citybike • www.lahemaa.ee; www.citybike.ee*

Lahemaa National Park

4 Tartu

Tartu is a historic university town, where neoclassical collegiate buildings coexist with Gothic churches and leafy parks. It is also home to the Estonian National Museum, which holds the biggest collection of ethnographic artifacts in the country. *Map C2 • Bus from Tallinn bus station • Estonian National Museum: 735 0445; Open 11am–6pm Tue–Sun; Adm • www.visittartu.com*

Town Hall Square, Tartu

5 Haapsalu

A genteel 19th-century spa town once patronized by the Tsarist nobility,

Haapsalu remains one of Estonia's most charming coastal resorts. Downtown streets are characterized by traditional timber buildings and there are some fine sandy beaches within walking distance. ✎ *Map A2 • Bus from Tallinn bus station • www.haapsalu.ee*

6 Rakvere

One of northeastern Estonia's most picturesque provincial towns, Rakvere is dominated by its 14th-century castle. Climb the restored tower and stroll the battlements for a taste of medieval history. ✎ *Map C1 • Bus from Tallinn bus station • Rakvere Castle: 322 5500; Open 11am–7pm May–Sep • www.rakvere.ee*

7 Pärnu

A glorious 6-km- (3.7-mile-) long stretch of sandy beach is Pärnu's main attraction, the resort that dubs itself "Estonia's summer capital". Waterside parks, traditional wooden architecture and some good restaurants are additional reasons to visit. ✎ *Map B3 • Bus from Tallinn bus station • www.visitparnu.com*

8 Paldiski

Originally built by Peter the Great, the port of Paldiski was notorious as the site of a Soviet nuclear submarine base from the 1960s onwards. An eerie townscape of semi-derelict naval buildings bordered by dramatic coastal cliffs make for an unusual day out. ✎ *Map A1 • Train from Balti Jaam station • www.paldiski.ee*

9 Põltsamaa

The market town of Põltsamaa centres on one of the country's medieval strongholds – the ruins of Põltsamaa Castle. Built into the walls is the 14th-century town church, the tower of which once served as a fire platform for cannon. ✎ *Map C2 • Bus from Tallinn bus station • www.poltsamaa.ee*

Castle of the Order, Põltsamaa

10 Helsinki

A two-to-three hour journey across the Baltic Sea by ferry, Helsinki will appeal to anyone interested in Art Nouveau architecture, modern design and shopping. ✎ *Map B1 • Ferries operated by Lindaline; Viking; Eckerö; Tallink • www.visithelsinki.fi; www.lindaliini.ee; www.vikingline.ee; www.eckeroline.ee; www.tallink.ee*

Carry your passport as ID on the ferry to Helsinki.

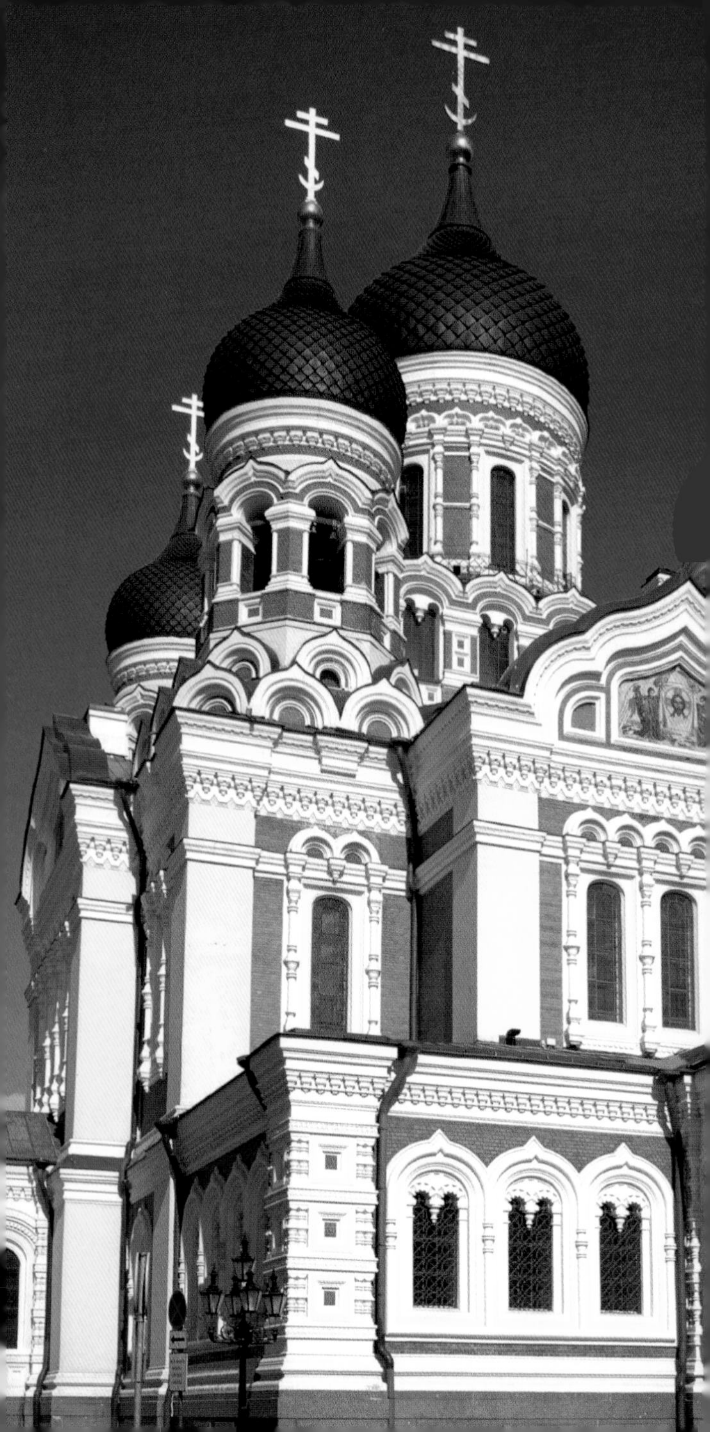

AROUND TALLINN

Left **Crest of Toompea Castle** Centre **Toompark** Right **Old Post Office**

Toompea (Castle Hill)

BRISTLING WITH CHURCH SPIRES AND MEDIEVAL TOWERS, *Toompea or "Castle Hill" has been at the political heart of Estonia ever since falling to the Danes in the 13th century. Successive Teutonic, Swedish and Russian rulers have used it as their power base, and it currently serves as home to the Estonian Parliament, several government ministries and both Lutheran and Orthodox cathedrals. Despite the concentration of so many state and religious institutions, Toompea is a surprisingly peaceful part of town, characterized by quiet pedestrianized alleys overlooked by pastel-hued mansions. Situated around the edges of the hill are several lookout points, each offering a panoramic view of the city below.*

View from Kohtuotsa Viewing Platform

Top 10 Sights

1. Dome Church
2. Orthodox Cathedral of Alexander Nevsky
3. Toompea Castle
4. Kohtuotsa Viewing Platform
5. Old Post Office
6. Kiek-in-de-kök
7. Toompark
8. Lindamägi
9. Museum of Occupations
10. The Danish King's Garden

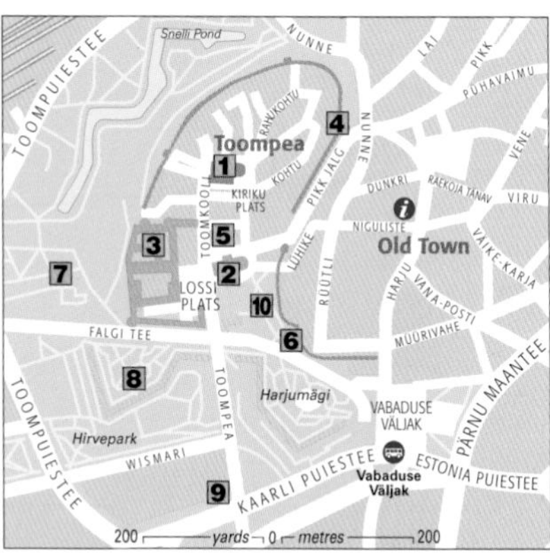

Preceding pages **Orthodox Cathedral of Alexander Nevsky**

1 Dome Church

A Gothic structure topped by an onion-shaped baroque belfry, the Dome Church seems more like a charming village chapel than Estonia's main Lutheran place of worship. Built by the Danes in 1219, it is believed to be the oldest surviving church in Estonia. It remained for centuries the most prestigious place in Tallinn to be buried, and the floor and walls of the nave are studded with grave plaques and funerary monuments. Prominent among these are the tombs of Pontus de la Gardie and Otto von Uexküll *(see pp18–19)*.

2 Orthodox Cathedral of Alexander Nevsky

Modelled on the Muscovite churches of the 17th century, the cathedral was built by Tallinn's Russian rulers in 1894. It is dedicated to Alexander Nevsky, the prince of Novgorod who defeated the Teutonic Knights on Lake Peipsi in 1242. Nevsky features prominently as the subject of frescoes and icons in the cathedral's interior.
Lossi plats 10 • Map H4 • 644 3484 • Open 8am–7pm

Orthodox Cathedral of Alexander Nevsky

Estonian Parliament, Toompea Castle

3 Toompea Castle

Situated on the hill's highest point, Toompea Castle occupies the site of the original fortress built by Tallinn's medieval rulers. However, the first thing you see when approaching from Lossi plats is the Neo-Renaissance administration building erected by the Russians in the 19th century. The Estonian Parliament sits in an assembly hall built inside the Castle courtyard. The older parts of the castle can be seen round the western side, most notably in the form of the slender Pikk Hermann tower – where an Estonian national flag flutters from the flagpole. *Lossi plats • Map G4 • 631 6345 • Open 10am–4pm Mon–Fri, adm with guided tour*

4 Kohtuotsa Viewing Platform

Most popular of the lookout points placed around the edge of Toompea Hill is the Kohtuotsa viewing platform, located at the end of Kohtu street. The parapet affords a wonderful view of Tallinn's Old Town, with the spires of the Oleviste, Niguliste and Holy Ghost churches soaring skywards in the foreground. Further east are the concrete, glass and steel towers of modern Tallinn, with a cluster of international hotels and corporate offices demonstrating how much the city has changed since the restoration of independence in 1991. *Kohtu • Map H3*

Deportations

Throughout the Soviet period Lindamägi hill served as a focus of remembrance for Estonians deported to Siberia in the 1940s. There were two waves of deportations (June 1941 and March 1949) involving over 30,000 people taken from all classes of Estonian society. From the late 1950s onwards, deportees were gradually allowed to return home.

5 Old Post Office

This pea-green baroque house was originally the home of Wolmar Anton von Schlippenbach (1653–1721), a Swedish officer who was captured by the Russians at the Battle of Poltava in 1709. Schlippenbach befriended Peter the Great, and both Peter and Empress Catherine stayed in his house after the fall of Tallinn to the Russians in 1710. The building serves as Toompea's post office, and visitors can admire the low-ceilinged, barrel-vaulted interior during working hours. *Lossi plats 4 • Map H4 • 646 6109 • Open 9am–5pm Mon–Fri*

6 Kiek-in-de-kök

Dating from 1475, this stout six-storey tower was built to provide a fire platform for the town's artillery batteries. The houses of the Old Town were visible from the tower's cannon ports, earning it the name of Kiek-in-de-kök (peek into the kitchen). A museum display inside includes weaponry, uniforms and a scale model of Tallinn's 16th-century fortifications. The views from the top-floor windows provide an opportunity to test whether the tower's name still holds true *(see pp16–17)*.

Kiek-in-de-kök

7 Toompark

The tree-lined alleyways and flowerbeds of Toompark were laid in the mid-19th century, when many defensive bastions were demolished to make way for a green belt of promenades. The park's central feature is the Snelli Pond, a lake formed from Tallinn's former moat. The pond gets its name from Johann Schnell, Tallinn's head gardener in the years before World War I. *Map G4*

Toompark

8 Lindamägi

A leafy park on the south side of Toompea, Lindamägi (Linda's Hill) gets its name from the statue placed at its summit in 1920. Sculpted by August Weizenberg, the statue depicts Linda, mother of folk hero Kalevipoeg *(see p35)*. According to legend, Lake Ülemiste on Tallinn's eastern outskirts was formed from the tears shed by Linda for her dead husband Kalev. Weizenberg's original statue has been moved to KUMU to protect it from the elements, and a faithful replica now guards the spot. *Map G4*

9 Museum of Occupations

Besides documenting both Nazi and Soviet occupations of the country, this museum also charts the patriotic upsurge that engineered the "Singing Revolution" of 1987–91. Archival newsreel footage on show here reveals just how important traditional song festivals were in nurturing a sense of national togetherness *(see pp20–21)*.

Museum of Occupations

10 The Danish King's Garden

Overlooked by three medieval towers and a surviving section of wall, this small stretch of lawn and shrubs marks the spot where the invading Danes are believed to have defeated local Estonian tribes in 1219. According to Danish lore, it was here that the Dannebrog (the Danish national flag) fell miraculously from the sky, inspiring the Christian Danes to victory over the Estonian pagans. *Lühike jalg 9A • Map H4 • Open daily 24 hours*

A Day on Toompea

Morning

There are two main routes to Toompea from Tallinn's Old Town: the first involves a gentle ascent of Pikk jalg (Long Leg); while the second is the steeper climb up the stepped alleyway called Lühike jalg (Short Leg). Either way you'll emerge out onto Lossi plats, site of both **Toompea Castle** and the candy-coloured **Alexander Nevsky Cathedral** *(see p69)*. Pause for coffee in the quirky **Bogapott** café *(see p73)* before heading towards Kiriku plats, site of the **Dome Church** *(see pp18–19)*. From here, a leisurely circuit of northern Toompea's cobbled streets should culminate with the panorama on offer at the **Kohtuotsa Viewing Platform** *(see p69)*. The nearby **Olematu Rüütel** restaurant *(see p73)* is the best place for lunch.

Afternoon

Retrace your steps to Lossi plats and explore the **Danish King's Garden** before continuing to the **Kiek-in-de-kök** cannon tower, site of an absorbing military history display. Kiek-in-de-kök is also the starting point of the tour of the **Bastion Tunnels** *(see p72)*, a warren of passageways located beneath Toompea's former gun positions. From here it is a short walk downhill to the **Museum of Occupations** – history enthusiasts could easily spend an hour or so here absorbing all the materials on display. Wind things up with a relaxing stroll through **Hirvepark** *(see p72)*, or an early-evening cocktail at the **Varblane** outdoor bar *(see p73)*.

Left **Hirvepark** Right **Steps leading up to Lühike jalg**

TOP 10 Best of the Rest

1 Pikk jalg

Stroll along this sloping cobbled street that runs below some of Toompea Hill's finest 19th-century mansions. Souvenir sellers dressed in the Estonian national costume line the way *(see pp10–11)*.

2 Lühike jalg

This crooked stepped street is one of Tallinn's most picturesque, climbing past baroque dwellings before passing beneath the 15th-century Väravatorn (Gate Tower). *Map H4*

3 Kuberneri aed

Laid out in the 1820s, the Governor's Garden features an avenue of lime trees, a rose garden and pleasant views towards Lindamägi hill. *Map H4*

4 Toom-kooli Viewing Platform

Set beside the north wall of Toompea Castle, this secluded terrace provides panoramic views of Tallinn's western suburbs, with the trees, flowerbeds and sports facilities of Toompark laid out immediately below. *Map H4*

5 The Stenbock House

This lemon-yellow palace originally served as the Tallinn pied-à-terre of the landowning Stenbock family. It is currently the office of Estonia's prime minister. The porticoed façade is best viewed from Toompark below. *Rahukohtu 3 • Map H3*

6 The German Ambassador's Residence

This 17th-century house is one of Toompea's best-preserved residences. The Neo-Classical portico was added in the early 1800s. *Lossi plats • Map H4*

7 The Bastion Tunnels

Running under the south-eastern side of Toompea, these tunnels were built by the Swedes in the 17th century so that they could service their hillside gun positions unobserved by besiegers. *Komandandi 2 • Map H4 • 644 6686 • Open 10:30am–5:30pm Tue–Sun • Adm • www.linnamuuseum.ee/kok*

8 Monument to 20 August 1991

Besides the junction of Toompea and Falgi streets is a large granite boulder engraved with "20.VIII 1991." The date commemorates Estonia's declaration of independence from the Soviet Union. *Map H4*

9 Hirvepark

Hirvepark (deer park) occupies a dried-out section of Tallinn's former moat. The name refers to the animals kept in an enclosure here in the 1930s. *Map G5*

10 Monument to Kristjan Raud

Dedicated to Kristjan Raud (1865–1943), the artist famous for illustrating the 1935 edition of *Kalevipoeg*, this memorial features angular reliefs that echo motifs from his work. *Map G5*

Tours of the Bastion Tunnels (1hr 20min; booking in advance) commence at Kiek-in-de-kök.

Price Categories

For a three course meal for one with half a bottle of wine (or equivalent meal), taxes and extra charges.	
€	under €15
€€	€15–€25
€€€	€25–€35
€€€€	€35–€50
€€€€€	over €50

Left **Bogapott**

TOP 10 Restaurants, Bars and Cafés

1 Bogapott
With wooden benches filling a courtyard lined with window-box flowers, Bogapott is a most relaxing café. *Pikk jalg 9 • Map H4 • 631 3181 • Open 10am–7pm Mon–Sat, 10am–5pm Sun*

2 Pika jala kohvik
This café offers both hot and alcoholic drinks, alongside salads, soups and ciabatta sandwiches. *Pikk jalg 16 • Map H4 • 648 1428 • Open 9am–8pm*

3 Olematu Rüütel
A chic restaurant serving upmarket Estonian fare, with duck and venison on the menu. There's also a wine-tasting room. *Kiriku põik 4a • Map H3 • 631 3827 • Open 9am–11pm • €€€€*

4 Luscher & Matiesen
An impressive wine list and occasional live music make this café a great stop off for daytime refreshments. *Kohtu 12 • Map H3 • 5691 2910 • Open 9am–11pm*

5 Syrtaki
Known for its grilled meats and gyros-style kebabs, this Greek-themed restaurant has dining rooms adorned with murals of the Aegean islands. *Piiskopi 1 • Map H4 • 644 6076 • Open 11am–10pm Mon–Fri, 10am–11pm Sat, 10am–7pm Sun • €€€*

6 Kiek-in-de-kök Café
Although nothing more than a counter selling coffee, soft drinks, muffins and pastries, this café enjoys a remarkable setting atop the barrel-shaped tower *(see p16)*.

7 Maias Munk Almond Stall
Pick up a bag of roast almonds, coated in a mix of ginger and other spices, from this sweets' stall just outside the Dome Church. *Kiriku plats*

8 La Boheme
Located inside the Stackelberg Hotel, this café-brasserie offers bruschettas, pasta dishes and tempting desserts. *Paldiski mnt 1 • Map G4 • 660 0711 • Open noon–10pm*

9 Varblane
An open-air lounge-bar just below Kiek-in-de-kök tower, "The Sparrow" is a popular summer spot to indulge in cocktails and hookah pipes. *Harjumägi • Map H4 • 5625 6444 • Open 10am–3am*

10 Karoliina
Housed in a tunnel-like passage driven into the hillside, Karoliina provides an atmospheric setting for an intimate drink. *Harjumägi • Map J4 • 631 0505 • Open 11am–11pm*

Left **View from Oleviste Church** Right **Passion Altar, Niguliste Church**

The Old Town

FEW PLACES IN NORTHERN EUROPE *can match Tallinn's Old Town when it comes to the sheer number of medieval buildings still looming above its streets. With a cluster of defensive towers and church spires dating from the same epoch, it could almost be the set for an epic fantasy film. Gaps between the Gothic buildings have been filled in with baroque town houses and 19th-century apartment blocks to produce a visually stunning ensemble. The Old Town is very much the legacy of the mercantile culture that made medieval Tallinn rich. While nobles and priests lived on Toompea, traders and artisans settled in the town below, building tall gabled houses that were used as storehouses and shops as well as dwellings. With a seemingly random street plan of cobbled thoroughfares, Tallinn's Old Town invites hours of aimless strolling.*

Epping Tower, City Walls

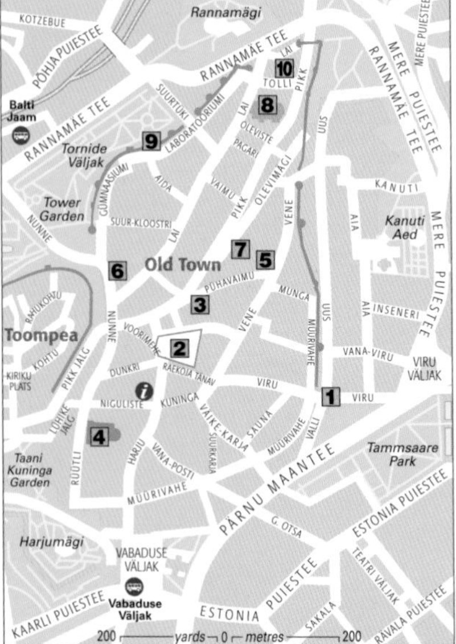

TOP 10 Sights

1. Viru Gate
2. Town Hall Square
3. Church of the Holy Ghost
4. Niguliste Church
5. City Museum
6. NUKU Puppet Museum
7. House of the Blackheads
8. Oleviste Church
9. The City Walls
10. The Three Sisters

1 Viru Gate

Consisting of two slender towers on either side of a busy shopping street, Viru Gate is one of Tallinn's most instantly recognizable visual features. Dating from the 14th century, the towers are all that remain of a much more complex system of fortifications, which originally comprised a bigger gate and drawbridge at the front and a huge rectangular tower at the back *(see pp16–17)*.

Clock, Church of the Holy Ghost

2 Town Hall Square

Lined with impressive town houses, Town Hall Square is where most of the Old Town's meandering streets meet. Dominating the square is the Town Hall itself, a handsome limestone building dating back to the 14th century. It is worthwhile to scale the Hall's spindly tower, where a lookout point just beneath the summit provides a view of the Old Town's sweeping labyrinthine streets. Still serving customers after more than six centuries, the Town Hall Pharmacy in the square's northwestern corner is one of Europe's oldest *(see pp8–9)*. *Town Hall Tower: Open 11am–6pm May–Sep • Adm*

3 Church of the Holy Ghost

With a stepped gable and an octagonal spire, this 13th-century structure is Tallinn's most captivating church. On the wall above the entrance is Tallinn's oldest clock, decorated with a golden sun motif by 17th-century artist Christian Ackermann. Inside, Bernt Notke's Holy Ghost altar of 1483 has a central panel crowded with painted statuettes of saints – a cloaked figure kneeling in front of the Virgin Mary is thought to be a portrait of the man who ordered the work, Tallinn mayor Derick Hagenbeck *(see pp8–9)*.

4 Niguliste Church

Dedicated to the patron saint of sailors, the Niguliste or St Nicholas' Church was for centuries the favoured place of worship among Tallinn's merchant classes. Much of the church was complete by the 15th century, although the two-tiered baroque belfry was added later. No longer a working church, the Niguliste is now a museum of sacral art, with Bernt Notke's *Danse Macabre* fresco among its highlights *(see pp12–13)*.

Town Hall Square

Marzipan

Made from almond paste and sugar, marzipan has been a Tallinn speciality since medieval times. Such was its ceremonial importance that marzipan moulds were once commissioned from celebrated 16th-century sculptor Arent Passer. Today, marzipan figures are sold as souvenirs and marzipan makers can be seen at work behind the counter of the Maiasmokk café *(see p11)*.

5 City Museum

This museum tells the story of Tallinn in an entertaining and accessible style. Mannequins dressed in straw boaters and summer dresses recall the 19th-century growth of tourism, when Tallinn became a popular beach resort among Baltic aristocrats and Russian civil servants. On the top floor, a wall of Nazi and Communist posters made by Estonia's 20th-century occupiers conveys a chilling sense of totalitarian coercion *(see pp14–15)*.

6 NUKU Puppet Museum

One of Tallinn's most colourful museum collections celebrates the history of the NUKU Puppet Theatre, founded by children's theatre veteran Ferdinand Veike in 1952. Veike's own puppets, frequently based on the heroes and maidens of Estonian folk tales, also figure in the display. There's an exhibition of marionettes from around the world, and a "Chamber of Horrors" full of dancing skeletons and pale-skinned beauties reclining in coffins.

Lai 1 • Map H3 • 667 9555 • Open 10am–7pm Tue–Sun • Adm • www.nuku.ee

Puppet on display, NUKU

House of the Blackheads

7 House of the Blackheads

The guild of Tallinn's bachelor merchants, the Brotherhood of the Blackheads *(see p11)* bought this building in 1517 to serve as a venue for their receptions and banquets. The profile of the Blackheads' patron, St Maurice, features prominently on the studded main doorway. The façade is covered in reliefs executed by Arent Passer in the 1590s: highlights include the portrayals of King Sigismund of Sweden and Queen Anna just above the first floor windows.

8 Oleviste Church

This lofty and serene place of worship started out as the church of Tallinn's Scandinavian community. The Church was named in honour of St Olaf, the 11th-century Norwegian king who supervised Norway's conversion to Christianity. A huge programme of expansion was undertaken in the 15th century, when the nave took on its current high-ceilinged form. The end of the century also saw the construction of the spire, which at 159 m (522 ft) was one of the wonders of the world then. *Steeple open 10am–6pm Apr–Oct • Adm*

9 The City Walls

Well over half of Tallinn's medieval walls are still intact and pinnacled towers and gateways still stand guard over most entrances to the Old Town. Built in stages from the 13th century onwards, they were constructed from the local pale grey limestone. Specific guilds were charged with the manning and supplying of specific towers, involving the whole population's readiness for defence. Clamber up the steep steps of the Nuns' Tower or the Hellemann Tower to experience Tallinn's fortifications from the inside *(see pp16–17)*.

10 The Three Sisters

Of all Tallinn's late-Gothic houses, the Three Sisters *(see p10)* are the most frequently photographed. Standing together on the corner of Pikk and Tolli streets, they were used as warehouses as well as dwellings, and loading hatches can still be seen running up the centre of each façade. Painted in bright hues of yellow, apricot and peach, the restored buildings are now home to the five-star Three Sisters hotel *(see p112)*.

The Three Sisters

A Day in Tallinn's Old Town

Morning

Observe the comings and goings at the bustling Town Hall Square from the terrace of **Kehrwieder** café *(see p85)* before heading up **Pikk** *(see pp10–11)*, the Old Town's most characteristic street. Savour views of Tallinn and its port from the summit of **Fat Margaret**, home to the **Maritime Museum** *(see p10)*. Return towards the square along Lai, where some of Tallinn's most memorable Gothic buildings are located. Visit the **Niguliste Church** *(see pp12–13)* to admire the best of Tallinn's medieval art before stopping off at **Fish & Wine** *(see p83)* for lunch.

Afternoon

After lunch, make your way to the **City Museum** *(see pp14–15)* to get the low-down on Tallinn's history. A stroll along the cobbled alley of Müürivahe will take you beneath a surviving stretch of medieval wall – scale the **Hellemann Tower** *(see p17)* and admire contemporary works exhibited in its top-floor art gallery. Then head to Katariina Käik *(see p58)* to explore the open studios and craft shops. The nearby **Chocolaterie Pierre** *(see p85)* is the ideal place to linger over coffee and a chocolate truffle. Once revived, head across the Old Town to the **Tornide väljak** park *(see p16)* to see the evening sun on Tallinn's crimson topped towers. Finish the day with a meal at **Ribe** *(see p82)*, followed by cocktails and live jazz in **Clazz** *(see p86)*.

Left **Museum of Applied Art & Design** Centre **Dominican Monastery** Right **Theatre & Music Museum**

Top 10 Best of the Rest

1 Theatre & Music Museum

Partly housed in a surviving medieval tower, this museum holds a collection of musical instruments through the ages. *Müürivahe 12 • Map J4 • 644 6407 • Open 10am–6pm Wed–Sat • Adm*

2 Maritime Museum

This fascinating array of model ships and nautical instruments is displayed in the 16th-century tower known as Fat Margaret *(see p10)*.

3 Dominican Monastery

Built by the Dominicans in the 13th century, central Tallinn's largest monastery complex was burned down during Protestant riots in 1524. Reopened in the 1950s, it now houses a museum of medieval stone carving. *Vene 16 • Map J3 • 515 5489 • Open mid-Jun–mid-Sep: 10am–5pm Tue–Sun • Adm*

4 Health Museum

The Health Museum offers an entertaining display of body parts in plastic-model form. Didactic diagrams and grisly photographs deal with social issues such as alcohol and drug abuse. *Lai 28 • Map J3 • 641 1730 • Open 11am–6pm Tue–Sat • Adm*

5 The Great Guild

This Gothic building served for centuries as the headquarters of the Great Guild of Tallinn's merchants. It is now used as an exhibition space by the Estonian History Museum *(see p11)*.

6 Transfiguration Church

Built by the Cistercian order, this church served as a barracks before being handed to an Orthodox community. The carved iconostasis is its main highlight. *Suur-kloostri 14-1 • Map J3 • 646 4003*

7 Museum of Applied Art and Design

A 17th-century granary houses this colourful collection, telling the history of Estonian design from its Pre-World War I beginnings. *Lai 17 • Map J2 • 627 4600 • Open 11am–6pm Wed–Sun • Adm*

8 St Nicholas's Orthodox Church

Built along neoclassical lines, this is one of Tallinn's more atmospheric churches. Glittering side altars date from 1688, when they were made for an older church that stood on this site. *Vene 24 • Map K3 • Open 11am–4pm*

9 The Epping Tower

The Epping Tower displays medieval arms and armour, including a full-size replica of a *ballista* – a huge crossbow used for shooting darts *(see p17)*.

10 Adamson-Eric Museum

Estonia's most versatile 20th-century artist, Adamson-Eric was equally at home whether painting in oils or designing metal jewellery. This museum presents an overview of his career. *Lühike jalg 3 • Map H4 • 644 5838 • Open 11am–6pm Wed–Sun • Adm*

Left **Houses of the Church Elders** Centre **The Russian Embassy** Right **Doorway at Suur-karja 1**

Top 10 Historic Houses

1 Doorway at Suur-karja 1
The ornate door at the start of Suur-karja is a fine example of baroque woodcarving in the city. The 17th-century building it belonged to was demolished in 1904, but the doorway was retained and re-inserted into the new building. *Map J4*

2 The House at Saiakang 4
Jutting out into the alleyway that runs between Town Hall Square and Pikk, this salmon-pink house is one of the most photogenic in the city. *Map J3*

3 The Russian Embassy
Designed by Jacques Rosenbaum, this Art Nouveau building is encrusted with fish, gargoyles, nymphs and a frock-coated gentleman wearing a lorgnette. *Pikk 21 • Map J3*

4 The House at Tolli 8
This is one of the many Tallinn addresses associated with Peter the Great, although the actual house in which the Tsar stayed burned down in 1757. The neoclassical mansion that replaced it served as Tallinn's Customs House. *Tolli 8 • Map J2*

5 The Three Brothers
These three tall buildings are medieval merchants' houses, each with loading hatches high up in the gables. The cast-iron lamps, added in the 19th century, are another distinctive local feature. *Lai 38-40 • Map J2*

6 Linnateater
Tallinn's Municipal Theatre occupies a most elegant late-Gothic house in the city. Pay a visit to the theatre café in order to peek inside the beautifully preserved entrance hall.
Lai 23 • Map J2

7 Houses of the Church Elders
The hauling hooks of these Gothic merchants' houses jut out just below roof level. The families who lived here were connected with the nearby Niguliste Church.
Rüütli 12 & 12a • Map H4

8 Hinse van Bremen's House
Built by merchant Hinse van Bremen in the 14th century, and lived in by several city mayors, this pointy-gabled house is an exemplary piece of late-medieval Tallinn architecture.
Vene 23 • Map K3

9 Kinomaja
Set apart by its green and red colour scheme, this mansion built in Dutch Renaissance style serves as home to the Estonian Film-makers' Union, and shows international art movies in its cinema. *Uus 23 • Map K3*

10 The Lithuanian Embassy
One of Tallinn's finest baroque town houses, this building was originally used by city councillors as a flax warehouse. The crests of three aldermen can be seen above the door. *Uus 3 • Map K3*

Left **Kuldse Notsu Kõrts** Right **Von Krahli Aed**

TOP 10 Estonian Restaurants

1 Balthasar
One of Tallinn's oldest restaurants, Balthasar serves up steak, game and fish dishes in timber-beamed chambers. *Raekoja plats 11 • Map J3 • 627 6400 • Open noon–midnight • €€€€*

2 Kuldse Notsu Kõrts
The piglet on the restaurant's logo accurately indicates the menu's affinity with pork dishes. *Dunkri 8 • Map J3 • 628 6567 • Open noon–11pm • €€€*

3 Kaerajaan
An ideal square-side location where pork, herring and duck dishes are prepared with imagination but remain true to Estonian traditions. *Raekoja plats 17 • Map J3 • 615 5400 • Open 11am–11pm • €€€€*

4 Mekk
A pioneer in the field of modern Estonian cuisine, Mekk juxtaposes traditional cuts of fish, duck and beef with exotic spices and vegetables. *Suur-karja 17/19 • Map J4 • 680 6688 • Open noon–11pm Mon–Sat • €€€€*

5 Olde Hansa
Tallinn's prime "medieval restaurant" excels in dishes such as pork in beer and sausages made from elk and boar. *Vana turg 1 • Map J3 • 627 9020 • Open 11am–midnight • €€€€*

6 Peppersack
Peppersack offers a medieval-themed menu of duck, pork and fish. Guests are also entertained with sword fights. *Viru 2 • Map J4 • 646 6800 • Open noon–midnight, sword fights 8pm onwards Tue–Sat • €€€€*

7 Ribe
Classic Estonian dishes such as duck, halibut and roast pork, presented in a modern European way. *Vene 7 • Map J3 • 631 3084 • Open noon–11pm • €€€€*

8 Stenhus
Sample haute cuisine Estonian style at Stenhus, a Baltic-French fusion restaurant with a seasonally changing menu. *Pühavaimu 13/15 • Map J3 • 699 7780 • Open noon–11pm • €€€€€*

9 Vanaema juures
As cosy as the name (which means "At Grandma's") suggests, this restaurant serves up delicious Estonian fare, from roast boar to freshwater fish. *Rataskaevu 10/12 • Map H3 • 626 9080 • Open noon–10pm Mon–Sat, noon–6pm Sun • €€€*

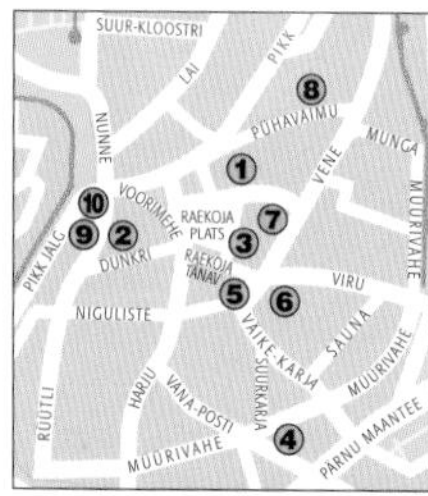

10 Von Krahli Aed
Tuck into duck, beef and pork dishes at candlelit Von Krahli Aed. The menu also caters for vegetarians. *Rataskaevu 8 • Map H3 • 626 9088 • Open noon–midnight Mon–Sat, noon–6pm Sun • €€€*

Price Categories

For a three course meal for one with half a bottle of wine (or equivalent meal), taxes and extra charges.

€	under €15
€€	€15–€25
€€€	€25–€35
€€€€	€35–€50
€€€€€	over €50

Left **Bonaparte** Right **Chakra**

TOP 10 International Restaurants

1 African Kitchen
Tuck into couscous dishes and spicy stews in this stylish place, with cushion-strewn benches, funky lanterns and a long cocktail list. *Uus 32 • Map K2 • 644 2555 • Open noon–midnight Sun–Thu, noon–2am Fri & Sat • €€€*

2 La Bottega
This restaurant serves the best in Italian cuisine from bruschettas to Florentine T-bones and a wide array of pasta dishes. *Vene 4 • Map J3 • 627 7733 • Open noon–11pm Mon–Thu, noon–midnight Fri & Sat, 1pm–10pm Sun • €€€*

3 Bonaparte
One of Tallinn's most elegant French restaurants, Bonaparte boasts a menu of classic duck, lamb and steak dishes. *Pikk 45 • Map J2 • 646 4444 • Open noon–midnight Mon–Sat • €€€€*

4 Chedi
Chedi's dim sum menu is the best in the Baltics and the seafood is outstanding. *Sulevimägi 1 • Map J2 • 646 1676 • Open noon–11pm Mon–Thu, noon–midnight Fri & Sat, 1pm–10pm Sun • €€€€€*

5 Controvento
Occupying a medieval house, this Italian restaurant serves superb pizzas and pastas. *Katariina käik • Map J3 • 644 0470 • Open noon–10:45pm • €€€€*

6 Elevant
Look out for some unusual choices of meat such as moose and boar, alongside plenty of vegetarian options at this relaxing Indian restaurant. *Vene 5 • Map J3 • 631 3132 • Open noon–11pm • €€€€*

7 Fish & Wine
Enjoy fish and seafood with a Mediterranean slant, served up with style in the chic Pegasus building. *Harju 1 • Map J4 • 662 3013 • Open 11:30am–11pm Mon–Thu, 11:30am–1am Fri–Sat, 11:30am–9pm Sun • €€€*

8 Museum
Risottos, pastas and sushi are the hallmarks of this cosmopolitan restaurant-cum-lounge bar. *Vana-Viru 14 • Map K3 • 646 0901 • Open noon–11pm Sun–Thu, noon–1am Fri & Sat • €€€€*

9 Must Lammas
Georgian favourites such as skewer-grilled kebabs, walnut-flavoured stews and cheesy *khachapuri* bread are served up with extra attention to detail. *Sauna 2 • Map J4 • 644 2031 • Open noon–11pm Mon–Sat, noon–6pm Sun • €€€€*

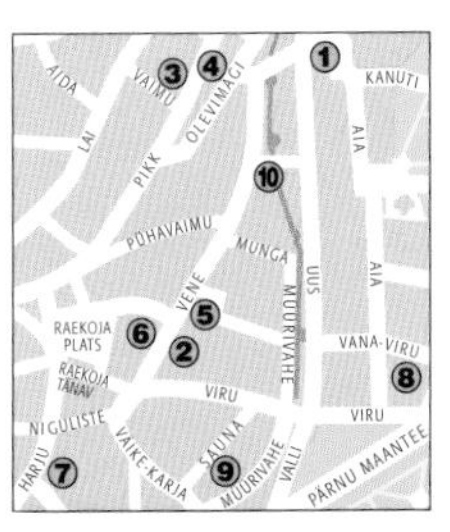

10 Chakra
Classic Indian dishes served in a trio of barrel-vaulted brick chambers hung with oriental textiles. *Bremeni käik 1 • Map K3 • 641 2615 • Open noon–midnight Sun–Thu, noon–1am Fri & Sat • €€€€*

Left **Bonaparte Deli** Centre **Felt hats on display at Hindricus** Right **Counter at Maiasmokk**

Top 10 Shops

1 Rahva Raamat Bookshop
One of Estonia's oldest bookshops, this is a good place to seek out English-language fiction and illustrated books about Estonian culture. *Parnu mnt 10 • Map M4 • Open 9am–7pm Mon–Fri, 10am–5pm Sat, 10am–4pm Sun*

2 Bonaparte Deli
A few doors along from Bonaparte restaurant *(see p83)*, the same company's delicatessen shop is a great place to pick up handmade truffles, quiches and freshly baked bread. *Pikk 47 • Map J2 • Open 10am–7pm Mon–Sat*

3 Eesti kasitöö
The official outlet for the Estonian Folk Art Union, this shop sells traditional hand-woven textiles. *Pikk 22 • Map J3 • Open 10am–6pm Mon–Sat, 10am–5pm Sun*

4 Hindricus
A shop stocking quality Estonian handicrafts made by local artisans, including felt hats, woollen socks and medieval-inspired jewellery. *Lühike jalg 2 • Map H4 • 660 5203 • Open 10am–6pm Mon–Sat, 10am–4pm Sun*

5 Ingli ja nööbi pood
Situated right beneath the tower of the Church of the Holy Ghost, the tiny "Angel and Button Shop" sells wooden, ceramic and stained-glass angels, alongside buttons fashioned from native Estonian trees. *Puhavaimu 2 • Map J3 • Open 10am–6pm*

6 Maiasmokk
Handmade marzipan sweets and fancy chocolates fill the display cabinets of Maiasmokk café's sweet shop *(see p11)*.

7 Bogapott
A ceramic store with a difference, Bogapott offers the kind of artist-designed ware that deserves a place on the kitchen shelf. *Pikk jalg 9 • Map H4 • Open 10am–6pm Mon–Sat, 10am–5pm Sun*

8 Sepa Äri
This traditional ironmonger sells everything from door-knockers to garden furniture. Smaller items like cup holders, candlesticks and bottle openers make good souvenirs. *Olevimägi 11 • Map J2 • Open 10am–6pm Mon–Fri, 10am–5pm Sat, 10am–3pm Sun*

9 VeTa
For linen clothes that are contemporary and stylish rather than folksy, head for VeTa. The clothes on offer here will make good summer wear. *Pikk 6 • Map J3 • Open 10am–7pm*

10 Zizi
Zizi carries a broad range of pure linen products for the household – sheets, bedspreads, pillowcases and tea towels. Well worth picking up are the linen bath towels, whose mildly rough texture serves as a great way to exfoliate the skin. *Suur-karja 2 • Map J4 • Open 10am–6pm Mon–Sat, 10am–4pm Sun*

Left **C'est la Vie** Centre **Cakes and pastries, Mademoiselle** Right **Chocolaterie Pierre**

TOP 10 Cafés

1 Chocolaterie Pierre

This delightful café offers handmade chocolates and truffles alongside other tasty snacks such as quiches, sandwiches and soups. *Vene 6 • Map J3 • 641 8061 • Open 9am–11pm*

2 Anneli Viik

A smart, cosy café with only four tables, Anneli Viik offers a delicious range of chocolates made on the premises. *Pikk 30 • Map J3 • 644 4530 • Open 11am–7pm Sun–Thu, 11am–9pm Fri & Sat*

3 C'est La Vie

An Art Deco influenced establishment, C'est La Vie boasts shiny black furnishings, brass fittings and an excellent selection of bruschettas, cakes and fruity meringue pies. *Suur-karja 5 • Map J4 • 641 8048 • Open noon–11pm Sun–Thu, noon–1am Fri & Sat*

4 Elsebet

Occupying the same building as the Peppersack restaurant *(see p82)*, Elsebet is popular on account of its pastries, croissants and open sandwiches. *Viru 2 • Map J3 • 646 6995 • Open 8am–5pm Mon–Sat, 9am–5pm Sun*

5 Maiasmokk

Tallinn's oldest café is an oasis of olde worlde charm, with wood panelling, informal order-at-the-counter service and a menu of traditional Estonian *pirukas* (pies). The chocolate treats and cakes are top-notch *(see p11)*.

6 Mademoiselle

With a counter laden with scrumptious cakes and freshly baked pastries, it is difficult to walk past Mademoiselle without being tempted. *Pikk 29 • Map J3 • 664 8805 • Open 7am–9pm*

7 Kõrts Inn Krug

Located in the Town Hall, this café has an appropriately medieval atmosphere. Enjoy strong coffee with *pirukas* or a slice of cake. *Raekoja Plats 1 • Map J3 • 627 9020 • Open 8am–midnight daily*

8 Kehrwieder

Coffee, ice cream and cheesecakes are served in this café that features low ceilings, wooden floorboards and a jumble of old furniture. There is outdoor seating too. *Saiakang 1 • Map J3 • 5554 7436 • Open 8am–11pm Sun–Thu, 8am–1pm Fri & Sat*

9 Matilda

Matilda's flowery wallpaper and soft furnishings make it one of the Old Town's most soothing spots for coffee. The counter display of cakes is enticing. *Lühike jalg 4 • Map H4 • 681 6590 • Open 9am–7pm Mon–Sat, 9am–6pm Sun*

10 Saiakangi kohvik

Much loved by the locals, this traditional café offers a good choice of cakes, open sandwiches and quality coffee. *Saiakang 3 • Map J3 • 644 3055 • Open 9am–8pm Mon–Sat, 10am–6pm Sun*

Recommend your favourite café on **traveldk.com**

Left **Interior, Von Krahl** Centre **Osteria del Gallo Nero** Right **Musi**

Top 10 Bars

1 Levist valjas
An alternative bar in the Old Town where one can enjoy cheap beer and spirits among a friendly crowd. *Olevimagi 12 • Map J2 • 504 6048 • Open 3pm–3am Sun–Thu, 3pm–6am Fri & Sat*

2 Clazz
This basement bar hosts live jazz most nights, and soul-funk DJs at weekends. Food ranges from steaks to salads and there is a "night menu" of burgers and sandwiches. *Vana turg 2 • Map J4 • 627 9022 • Open nightly*

3 Depeche Mode
Named after the British electronic group of the 1980s, Depeche Mode's cellar rooms are decked with fake leather benches. Cocktails are named after their hits. *Voorimehe 4 • Map J3 • 631 4308 • Open noon–3am*

4 Deja Vu
Ideally located in the heart of the Old Town, Deja Vu offers top quality food and cocktails. Weekend DJ's, live acts and the open air terrace in summer add to its popularity. *Vana-Viru 8 • Map K3 • 688 4455 • Open noon–midnight Mon & Tue, noon–6am Wed–Sat, noon–5am Sun*

5 Embassy Lounge
Embassy Lounge makes its patrons feel at home with plush sofas, low-key lighting and background music. *Väike-Karja 1 • Map J4 • 641 2202 • Open 5pm–2am Sun–Thu, 5pm–5am Fri & Sat*

6 Osteria del Gallo Nero
Enjoy Italian wine and some delicious pasta dishes, cheese-and-salami platters and eat-in or take-out panini in this café-bar. *Rataskaevu 4 • Map J3 • 646 2107 • Open 10am–midnight*

7 Ice Bar
Decked out in a combination of whites and greys, the Ice Bar serves shots in tiny glasses that are made of ice. A great place to knock back a vodka. *Dunkri 4/6 • Map J3 • 697 7500 • Open 11am–11pm Sun–Thu, 11am–midnight Fri & Sat*

8 Butterfly Lounge
The cocktails at this award winning bar are superb. It hosts live acts and DJs on weekends and acoustic acts on the second Thursday of the month. *Vana-Viru 13 • Map K3 • 690 3703 • Open noon–midnight Mon & Tue, noon–2am Wed–Fri, 3pm–3am Sat*

9 Musi
A wide-ranging wine list is backed up with a Mediterranean-influenced menu of both meat and vegetarian dishes at Musi. *Niguliste 6 • Map J4 • 644 3100 • Open 5pm–midnight Mon–Sat*

10 Von Krahl
With exposed-brick interiors and a bohemian vibe, Von Krahl is a relaxed drinking venue most nights of the week and an alternative club on weekends. *Rataskaevu 10/12 • Map H3 • 626 9090 • Open nightly*

Left **Clayhills Gastropub** Right **Bar at Hell Hunt**

Top 10 Pubs

1 Beer House
A German-themed bar with a sausage and sauerkraut menu, Beer House is also a micro-brewery producing unfiltered brews. *Dunkri 5 • Map J3 • 644 2222 • Open 11am–midnight Sun–Thu, 11am–2am Fri & Sat*

2 Clayhills Gastropub
Clayhills boasts a menu of stylishly presented pub food with plenty of salads and pastas. *Pikk 13 • Map J3 • 641 9312 • Open 11am–midnight Sun–Tue, 11am–1am Wed–Thu, 11am–2am Fri & Sat*

3 Drink Bar & Grill
A wide choice of international beers have placed Drink Bar & Grill at the centre of Tallinn's social life. Quiz nights and comedy evenings maintain the sense of camaraderie. *Väike-karja 8 • Map J4 • 644 9433 • Open noon–midnight Sun–Thu, noon–3am Fri & Sat*

4 Hell Hunt
Sample a solid menu of hot meals and palatable own-brand beers at Hell Hunt. Outdoor seating in summer. *Pikk 39 • Map J4 • 681 8333 • Open noon–2am*

5 Karja Kelder
An old-fashioned cellar pub full of balustraded partitions and cosy corners. Food is inexpensive and there is a chance to catch live cover bands at weekends. *Väike-karja 1 • Map J4 • 644 1008 • Open 11am–midnight Sun–Mon, 11am–2am Tue–Thu, 11am–4am Fri & Sat*

6 Molly Malone's
Molly's is the place to enjoy a pint of Guinness or sample a range of Irish whiskeys. The menu features shepherd's pie and fish and chips. *Mündi 2 • Map J3 • 631 3016 • Open 10am–1am Sun–Thu, 9am–4am Fri & Sat*

7 Nimeta Baar
A long-standing favourite with Tallinn's English-speaking community, with a convivial atmosphere, nighttime DJs and a varied menu of food. *Suur-karja 4 • Map J4 • 641 1515 • Open 10am–4am*

8 St Patrick's
Cushioned benches and deep armchairs contrast with centuries-old stone walls here. International beers and affordable meals add to the appeal. *Suur-karja 4 • Map J4 • 641 8173 • Open 11am–2am Sun–Thu, 11am–4am Fri & Sat*

9 Texas Honky Tonk
Choose from an international selection of beers in this laid-back pub, with country-tinged music in the background. *Pikk 43 • Map J3 • 631 1755 • Open noon–midnight Sun–Thu, noon–1am Fri & Sat*

10 Valli Baar
Unchanged since it first opened in 1969, this local bar is a valued city relic. *Millimalikas* ("jellyfish" – a shot comprising sambuca, tequila and tabasco sauce) is the standard order. *Müürivahe 14 • Map J4 • Open noon–2am Mon–Sat, noon–midnight Sun*

Left **Church of St Simeon and the Prophetess Hanna** Right **The Viru Hotel**

The New Town

RUNNING SOUTH AND EAST OF THE OLD TOWN *is Tallinn's main business district, a bustling area of offices, government ministries and shopping malls. The area first took shape during the 19th century when the Old Town no longer had enough room to accommodate the apartment blocks, factories and theatres that a growing city required. This part of town acquired a hard-nosed commercial character with the construction of the Rotermann Quarter, a cluster of workshops and storehouses that is today a focus of inner-city renovation and renewal. The 20th century saw the emergence of Vabaduse väljak, the square where many prestigious buildings were located. Towards the end of the 20th century this part of Tallinn became the site of high-rise hotels and corporate headquarters, earning it the title of Estonian Manhattan.*

Independence Monument

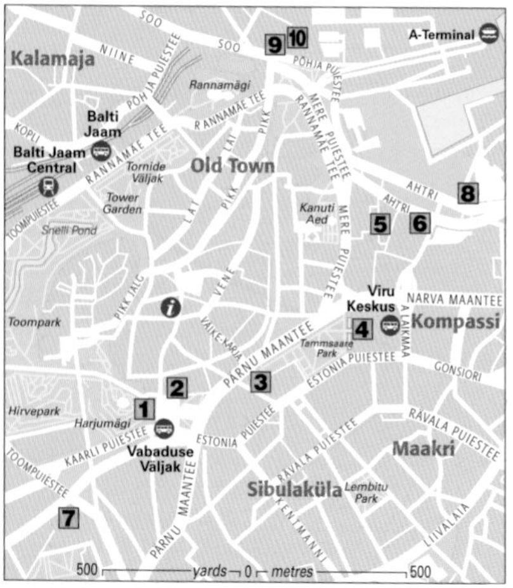

Top 10 Sights

1. Independence Monument
2. Tallinn Art Hall
3. Estonian Drama Theatre
4. The Viru Hotel
5. The Rotermann Quarter
6. The Architecture Museum
7. Estonian National Library
8. Church of St Simeon and the Prophetess Hanna
9. The Culture Cauldron
10. Contemporary Art Museum of Estonia

Estonian Drama Theatre

1 Independence Monument

A 24-m (79-ft) high pillar topped by a cross, this monument was erected in 2009 to honour those who fell during the Estonian War of Independence of 1918–20. This was a time when the fledgling state had to beat back both invading Bolsheviks and Baltic Germans to safeguard its independence. The cross at the top of the monument is modelled on the Estonian Cross of Victory, the service medal awarded to veterans of the independence campaign. Wreaths and flowers are regularly laid at the base of the monument. *Vabaduse väljak • Map H4*

2 Tallinn Art Hall

Built in 1934 by architect Edgar-Johan Kuusik, this is a fine example of Estonian inter-war architecture, with a portal framed by statues symbolizing the arts. The gallery played an important cultural role during the Soviet period, when the edgy exhibitions held here were frequently at odds with the official policies of Moscow-based art bureaucrats. The gallery's basement café, Kuku, was a notorious haunt for non-conformist intellectuals – as well as the KGB informants who listened in on their conversations. Today the gallery remains a bastion of culture, hosting exhibitions by contemporary Estonian artists. *Vabaduse väljak 6 • Map J4 • 644 2818 • Open noon–6pm Wed–Sun • Adm • www.kunstihoone.ee*

3 Estonian Drama Theatre

Originally built in 1910, Tallinn's prime drama venue is an outstanding example of the so-called national-romantic style of architecture that became popular right across the Baltic and Nordic countries in the years just before World War I. The style was characterized by its use of motifs drawn from folk craftsmanship. The steep, shingled roofs take their cue from the timber-built farmsteads common to north-European villages, while the reliefs and runic inscriptions on the façade are a clear reference to Teutonic and Scandinavian myth. *Pärnu mnt 5 • Map K4*

4 The Viru Hotel

Completed in 1970, the Viru Hotel was built by Finnish engineers to accommodate the increasing number of tourists arriving from Finland and soon gained a reputation for being the most westernized hotel in the Soviet Union. The Viru's other claim to fame during the Soviet era was its place in the black-market trade in jeans. Finnish tourists and business visitors frequently arrived with a spare pair or two in their luggage. *Viru väljak 4 • Map L4*

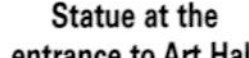

Statue at the entrance to Art Hall

The Estonian War of Independence (1918–20)

Estonia declared its independence on 24 February 1918, but spent the next two years fighting off invasions before freedom was finally secured. Initially fighting alone, it was subsequently aided by the British navy and volunteers from Finland. Every town square in the country boasts a monument to this defining moment.

5 The Rotermann Quarter

This area of 19th-century warehouses has become a major focus of urban renewal initiatives. Several warehouses have been refurbished, and modern buildings have sprung up in their midst, creating a contemporary city-centre space for chic shops, cafés and clubs. The area gets its name from Christian Abraham Rotermann, who opened one of Tallinn's first department stores in 1828. Rotermann constructed workshops and warehouses to feed his shop floor with goods – thereby creating the quarter that today bears his name. *Map L3*

6 The Architecture Museum

Opened in 1996, the Architecture Museum is located in a former salt storage depot built by Rotermann's son, Christian Barthold Rotermann. A striking limestone building that looks like a medieval fortress, the structure has been given a contemporary makeover. The museum's permanent collection consists of architectural plans and models of landmark buildings. Seasonal exhibitions focus on particular architects and styles. *Ahtri 2 • Map L2 • 625 7007 • Open 11am–6pm Wed–Sun • Adm • www.arhitektuurimuuseum.ee*

Church of St Simeon & the Prophetess Hanna

The Architecture Museum

7 Estonian National Library

Architect Raine Karp's National Library building makes impressive use of the local, pink-grey limestone. Hosting art displays on the ground floor is the main exhibition hall featuring a low arched ceiling supported by a squat central pillar. The Wiiralt Gallery on the third floor celebrates the work of graphic artist Eduard Wiiralt (1898–1954), whose distinctive drawings document his travels in inter-war France and North Africa. *Tõnismägi 2 • Map H5 • 630 7611 • Open 11am–8pm Mon–Fri, noon–7pm Sat*

8 Church of St Simeon and the Prophetess Hanna

Built in the 1750s, this pretty Orthodox church has a tapering belfry and a plump onion-shaped dome behind it. These external features were removed during the Soviet era, when the nave was turned into a sports hall. Reconstruction started in 2001 and St Simeon is once again a working church, its interior focusing on an iconostasis with vibrant holy images. ✆ *Ahtri 5 • Map M2 • Open 11am–5pm Tue–Fri, noon–2pm Sat, noon–3pm Sun*

9 The Culture Cauldron

Tallinn's newest venue for art exhibitions, club nights and avant-garde concerts, the Culture Cauldron occupies the renovated shell of a former municipal plant. The Cauldron's red-brick chimney is a much-loved local landmark. It was here that Soviet film director Andrei Tarkovsky filmed scenes from his 1978 classic *Stalker*, with the chimney marking the entrance to a forbidden zone guarded by UN troops. ✆ *Põhja 27a • Map K1 • www.kultuurikatel.org*

The Culture Cauldron

10 Contemporary Art Museum of Estonia

CAME was established in 2007 to serve as an alternative to "official" contemporary art institutions such as KUMU *(see pp26–9)* and the Tallinn Art Hall *(see p89)*. More of a cultural centre than a museum, CAME organizes exhibitions involving the younger generation of Tallinn's artists. Its stark grey halls provide the perfect environment for the edgy work that is usually on display. ✆ *Põhja 35 • Map K1 • 5663 6623 • Open 1pm–7pm Tue–Sun*

A Day in Tallinn's New Town

Morning

With its sights arranged in an arc around the Old Town, Tallinn's New Town is easy to explore. Vabaduse väljak, overlooked by the **Independence Monument** *(see p89)*, is a good place to get your bearings. From here stroll to the **Solaris** *(see p59)* and its rooftop **Komeet** café *(see p93)* for coffee and cakes. Afterwards, walk north via the **Estonian Drama Theatre** *(see p89)* and **The Estonia Concert Hall** *(see p92)* to Viru väljak, where shopping centres and high-rise hotels provide a flavour of contemporary Estonia. From here, you can dive into the **Rotermann Quarter** with its restored warehouses, snazzy shops and organic food market. Recharge your batteries with caffeine and a light snack at **Zebra Café** or a more relaxed lunch at **Spirit Café** *(see p93)*.

Afternoon

After lunch, walk west towards **The Culture Cauldron** and the Kalamaja district. With its former industrial buildings, humble wooden houses and modern luxury flats, this is a good place to sample the changing face of Tallinn. Continue to the western end of Kalamaja and visit the spooky **Patarei Prison** *(see p97)*, before finishing off the sightseeing with the vintage ships of the **Air Harbour Maritime Museum** *(see p97)*. Head back towards the city centre and an evening meal at **Ö** *(see p93)*, an award-winning pioneer of modern Estonian cuisine.

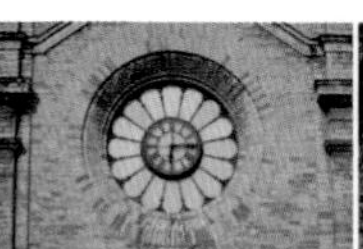

Left **The Estonia Concert Hall** Centre **St Charles's Church** Right **The 1905 Memorial**

Top 10 Best of the Rest

1 St Charles's Church
Completed in 1870, this Neo-Romanesque structure boasts a monumental depiction of Christ, painted by Estonian artist Johann Köler. *Kaarli pst • Map H5*

2 AHHAA Science Centre
Offering exhibits with an educative, scientific theme AHHAA houses a "4D" cinema, with chairs synchronized to vibrate in time to the on-screen action. *Vabaduse väljak 9 • Map J5 • 666 0066 • Open noon–8pm Mon–Fri, 10am–8pm Sat–Sun • Adm*

3 The City Council Building
The geometrically patterned brickwork of the façade is thrown into sharp relief as sunlight flits across this building's surface. *Vabaduse väljak 7 • Map J5*

4 St John's Church
Designed in 1860 by architect Christoph August Gabler, this Neo-Gothic church adds a touch of grace to what is a modern square. *Vabaduse väljak • Map J4*

5 The Boy of Bronze
The statue of this bronze youth honours the schoolboys who volunteered to fight in the Estonian War of Independence in 1918-20. *G Otsa • Map K4*

6 The Estonia Concert Hall
Built in 1913, the Estonia Concert Hall is the city's main concert venue, housing the National Opera in one wing and Estonian Symphony Orchestra in the other. *Estonia pst 4 • Map K4*

7 The 1905 Memorial
This monumental statue of a woman defending her wounded husband commemorates the anti-Tsarist demonstration of October 1905. *Pärnu mnt • Map K4*

8 The Church of Our Lady of Kazan
Dedicated to a famous lost icon of the Virgin Mary once kept in the Russian city of Kazan, this tulip-domed wooden church originally served as the chapel of the Tsarist imperial garrison. *Liivalaia 38 • Map L6 • Open 9am–5pm Sat & Sun*

9 The Linnahall
Opened in 1980 as the V.I. Lenin Palace of Culture and Sport, this concert hall is an icon among fans of modern architecture. *Mere pst 20 • Map B4*

10 Energy Discovery Centre
An enjoyable science museum, featuring endless halls of strange-looking machines for you to play around on. *Põhja pst. 29 • Map K1 • 715 2650 • Open 10am–6pm Mon–Fri, noon–5pm Sat • Adm*

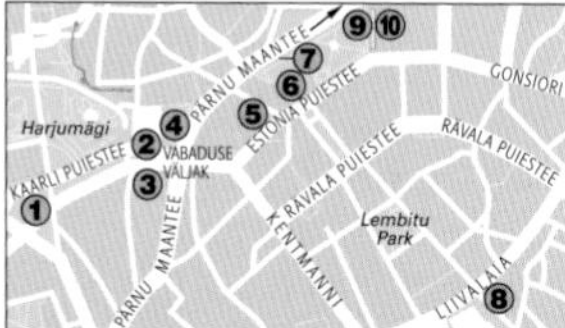

Left **Lounge 24**

Price Categories

For a three course meal for one with half a bottle of wine (or equivalent meal), taxes and extra charges.	
€	under €15
€€	€15–€25
€€€	€25–€35
€€€€	€35–€50
€€€€€	over €50

TOP 10 Restaurants and Cafés

1 Admiral
An old steamer tethered to the south side of Tallinn's main harbour is the setting for this restaurant specializing in Balkan grilled dishes. *Admiraliteedi bassein • Map A4 • 662 3777 • Open noon–11pm • €€€€*

2 Kohvik Moon
This stylish café-restaurant in the Kalamaja district serves up Baltic-Mediterranean fusion food with Russian and Polish recipes thrown in for good measure. *Võrgu 3 • Map A4 • 631 4575 • Open noon–11pm Tue–Sat, 1pm–9pm Sun • €€€*

3 Café VS
A brash DJ bar, home to some of the best Indian cuisine in the capital. *Pärnu mnt 28 • Map J5 • 627 2627 • Open 10am–midnight Mon–Thu, 10am–2am Fri, noon–2am Sat, noon–midnight Sun • €€€*

4 Zebra Café
Sleek furnishings and a varied menu of sushi, pastas, salads, cheesecakes and fancy gateaux make Zebra an instant hit with chic youngsters. *Narva mnt 7 • Map M3 • 610 9230 • Open 11am–11pm • €€€€*

5 Komeet
Admire the view through Komeet's floor-to-ceiling windows. The café's array of delectable cakes more than fits the setting. *Estonia pst 9 • Map K5 • 614 0090 • Open 10am–11pm Mon–Thu, 10am–midnight Fri & Sat, 10am–9pm Sun • €€*

6 Lido
On the first floor of the Solaris shopping centre, this caféteria boasts an extensive choice of Baltic dishes in large portions. *Estonia pst 9 • Map K5 • 609 3364 • Open 10am–10pm • €€*

7 Lounge 24
This rooftop bar and café prides itself on its extensive list of cocktails and toothsome menu of light bites. *Rävala pst 3 • Map L5 • 682 3424 • Open noon–midnight Sun–Wed, noon–2am Thu–Sat • €€€€*

8 Ö
Serving up rabbit, veal and game dishes, the award-winning Ö succeeds in taking Estonian country cooking and turning it into haute cuisine. *Mere pst 6e • Map L2 • 661 6150 • Open noon–11pm Mon–Thu, noon–midnight Fri & Sat, 1pm–10pm Sun • €€€€€*

9 Platz
Steak, duck and fish dishes are served in this stone warehouse in the Rotermann Quarter's main plaza. *Roseni 7 • Map L3 • 664 5086 • Open 5pm–midnight Mon–Sat • €€€€*

10 Spirit Café
With its matt-black floor and white art-gallery-style walls, Spirit is a chic place for a drink and also offers a cosmopolitan menu featuring pastas, salads and sushi. *Mere pst 6e • Map L2 • 661 6151 • Open noon–11pm Mon–Sat, 1–10pm Sun • €€€*

Recommend your favourite restaurant on ***traveldk.com***

ARDED
$ €
TROIKA
16

BAKU
BAKU
BAKU

Left **Air Harbour** Centre **Estonian History Museum** Right **Botanical Gardens**

Greater Tallinn

A PATCHWORK OF PARKS, SUBURBS *and renovated former industrial areas, Greater Tallinn contains plenty of interesting places for visitors. Its assets are its green spaces, with the leafy expanse of Kadriorg Park providing most in the way of recreational potential. Besides an abundance of trees and meadows, Kadriorg also offers a trio of unmissable art museums. Further east lie the stark ruins of Pirita Convent and the lush flora of the city's Botanical Gardens. Currently the focus of major redevelopment projects, the suburb of Kalamaja, northwest of the Old Town, is home to Tallinn's newest attractions – the Patarei Prison Museum and the Air Harbour Maritime Museum.*

Patarei Prison Museum

TOP 10 Sights

1. Patarei Prison Museum
2. Air Harbour Maritime Museum
3. Kadriorg Park
4. Kadriorg Palace Art Museum
5. Peter the Great's House
6. The Estonian Open-Air Museum
7. Estonian History Museum
8. Pirita Convent
9. Botanical Gardens
10. KUMU

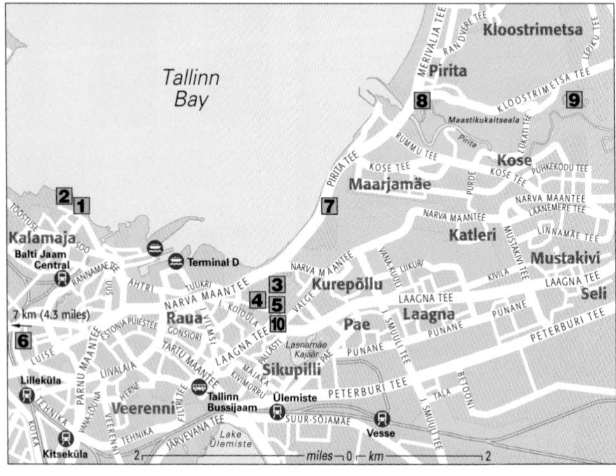

Preceding pages **Town Hall Square, Old Town**

1 Patarei Prison Museum

Initially an imperial Russian naval base, Patarei Prison also served as Tallinn's main high-security gaol from 1919 to 2004. It is not a museum in the traditional sense, but visitors can wander around the crumbling complex of grey brick buildings, exploring echoing corridors and peering into cells that look as if they were vacated only yesterday. *Kalaranna 2 • Map A4 • 504 6536 • Open noon–6pm Jun–Sep • Adm • www.patarei.org*

2 Air Harbour Maritime Museum

Located on the shore northwest of Patarei Prison, this is one of Tallinn's newest attractions. The museum's centrepiece is the concrete hangar that was built by the Russian navy in 1916 to house a squadron of seaplanes. In the centre of the hangar is Lembit, the sleek submarine made in British shipyards for the Estonian navy in 1937. Several vessels are moored in front of the building, with the ice-breaking steamer *Suur-Tõll* enjoying pride of place. *Küti 15a • Map A4 • 641 1408 • Open 10am–6pm Wed–Sun • Adm • www.meremuuseum.ee*

3 Kadriorg Park

The park's main attraction might be the terraced gardens that descend from east to west, but the broad stretches of landscaped meadow, crossed by tree-lined avenues are, arguably, its most charming feature. At the park's centre is Peter the Great's former palace, now the Kadriorg Palace Art Museum. The palace's ancillary buildings house museums, such as the Mikkel Museum and the Park Museum *(see pp22–3)*.

Rear Garden, Kadriorg Palace Art Museum

4 Kadriorg Palace Art Museum

Originally built to serve as Peter the Great's Baltic pied-à-terre, the maroon-and-ochre palace in the middle of Kadriorg Park now houses Estonia's national collection of foreign art. The display is strong on 19th-century Russian painting and Flemish still lifes, and there is also plenty of ceramics and silverware on show. A surviving feature from the Tsar's time is the Main Hall, decorated with stucco eagles *(see pp24–5)*.

Swan Lake, Kadriorg Park

Pirita Convent

The Bridgettine Convent at Pirita was one of 15th-century Tallinn's richest monastic communities. The Order welcomed both nuns and monks – although they lived in different wings of the convent and communication was strictly controlled. Destroyed in 1575, the Convent was re-established in 1994, and a new church erected next to the ruined original.

5 Peter the Great's House

This cottage was where the Russian Tsar resided while awaiting completion of his palace nearby. The interior contains furnishings and kitchenware from the 18th century, providing some idea of how Peter might have lived during his first visits to Tallinn. The Tsar captured the city from the Swedes in 1710 as part of the Great Northern War, a titanic struggle that lasted from 1699 to 1721 *(see pp22–3)*.

6 The Estonian Open-Air Museum

Situated to the west of the Old Town, the Open-Air Museum presents a marvellous opportunity to get a taste of Estonian rural life. Traditional farmsteads, schoolhouses and fire stations from all over the country have been transported and reassembled here in groups according to region. The most

Windmill, Open-Air Museum

Peter the Great's House, Catherine's room

striking aspect of the collection is the widespread use of timber, very often as the sole material in construction *(see pp30–31)*.

7 Estonian History Museum

Located in a 19th-century palace, the Estonian History Museum covers national affairs from the early 20th century onwards. Documentary footage of the national song festivals reveals the huge significance of these mass get-togethers in the Estonian psyche. The palace was earmarked as the future site of a museum of "Soviet Friendship" in the 1980s. One aspect of the project still survives – Evald Okas's Soviet-inspired propagandist frescoes in the banqueting hall.

Pirita tee 56 • Map D4 • 622 8610 • Bus 1, 8, 34A & 38 • Open 10am– 5pm Wed–Sun • Adm • www.ajaloomuuseum.ee

8 Pirita Convent

The seaside suburb of Pirita takes its name from the Swedish Saint Birgitta, founder of the Bridgettine Order of nuns. Founded in 1407, the convent was burned down by the invading forces of Ivan the Terrible in

1575. It survives today as a roofless shell, while traces of cells, kitchens and storehouses can be seen on either side. *Koostri tee 9 • Map E3 • 605 5044 • Bus 1, 8, 34A & 38 • Open 10am–6pm • Adm • www.piritaklooster.ee*

9 Botanical Gardens

Tallinn's Botanical Gardens, a spacious open park, boasts a rose garden, a plantation of lilac bushes from around the world and an alpine rock garden. Its central feature, the octagonal palm house, is connected to a series of green-houses filled with Mediterranean, Australasian and desert plants. *Kloostrimetsa tee 52 • Map F3 • 606 2666 • Bus 34A • Open 11am–6pm • Adm • www.tba.ee*

Botanical Gardens

10 KUMU

A grey limestone crescent emerging from a hill side, this building designed by Finnish architect Pekka Vapaavuori is the perfect counterpart to the art collection on display inside. The exhibition halls present a chronological journey through Estonian painting and sculpture, paying particular attention to the avant garde movements of the 1920s and 30s. The expressionist landscapes of Konrad Mägi and the angular cubist creations of Arnold Akberg are among KUMU's many highlights *(see pp26–9)*.

A Day in Kadriorg Park

Morning

Tram no. 1 and 3 trundle from Viru väljak to the park's main entrance in under 10 minutes – otherwise it is a brisk 2-km (1.3-mile) walk or cycle ride. Refresh yourself with tea or coffee at the serene **Park Café** *(see p101)* before heading up Weizenbergi, the tree-lined avenue that runs through **Kadriorg Park** *(see p97)* from west to east. The main sightseeing target here is the **Kadriorg Palace Art Museum** *(see p97)*, with its historic interiors and international art. Head next door to **The Mikkel Museum** *(see p22–3)* if you still have an appetite for old masters, otherwise take a stroll around the French-style geometric gardens behind the palace. Take time out for lunch at the **KUMU Café** *(see pp101)*, or find a dry stretch of grass on which to spread out a picnic blanket.

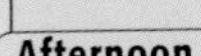

Afternoon

The **KUMU** art museum may take an hour or two of your sightseeing time – there are usually a couple of temporary exhibitions here besides the permanent collection. From here you can return towards the main entrance of the park via the ornamental gardens that descend west towards the **Swan Lake** *(see p23)*. The **Restoran & Spaghetteria Kadriorg** *(see pp101)* is a relaxing place for a meal. If time allows, stroll northeast towards the **Rusalka Memorial** *(see p23)* and the nearby dunes, where you can watch the sun set over Tallinn's port.

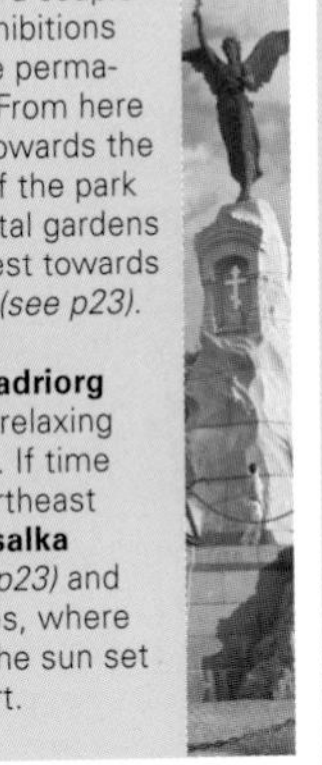

Left **Holidaymakers at Pirita beach** Right **Metsakalmistu cemetery**

Top 10 Best of the Rest

1 The Bronze Soldier

Honouring the Soviet soldiers who died in World War II, this memorial is a popular patriotic symbol for Tallinn's Russian community. *Filtri • Map B6*

2 The Tammsaare Museum

A museum dedicated to Anton Hansen Tammsaare (1878–1940), an Estonian novelist best known for his magnum opus *Tõde ja õigus* (Truth and Justice). *Koidula 12a • Map B5 • 601 3232 • Open 10am–5pm Wed–Mon • Adm*

3 Eduard Vilde Museum

This museum remembers Eduard Vilde (1865–1933) with a collection of original furnishings, manuscripts and personal effects *(see p23)*.

4 The Mikkel Museum

Housed in a building that once served as the Kadriorg Palace's kitchen, this museum contains paintings, ceramics and graphic art amassed by Johannes Mikkel *(see p23)*.

5 Song Bowl

Built in 1960, this stage hosts the mass choral festivals that play an important role in the Estonian cultural calendar *(see p55)*. *Narva mnt 95 • Map C4*

6 Soviet War Memorial

One of Tallinn's most prominent Soviet heirlooms, this needle-shaped obelisk is a memorial to the Red Army war dead of 1918–20 and 1941–45. *Pirita tee • Map D3 • Bus 1, 8, 34A & 38*

7 Pirita Beach

Stretching east from the mouth of the Pirita river, this lovely ribbon of silver sand runs for 3 km (2 miles). *Map D2 • Bus 1, 8, 34A & 38*

8 Metsakalmistu Cemetery

Many famous Estonian musicians and writers are buried in this beautiful graveyard. *Koostrimetsa tee • Map F2 • Bus no 34A*

9 Television Tower

Built in time for the Olympic Games in 1980, this 314-m (1030-ft) high tower looms above the Botanical Gardens. *Kloostrimetsa tee • Map F3*

10 Tallinn Zoo

Founded in 1937 for the baby lynx won by the Estonian Riflemen's Society at the World Championships in Helsinki, the zoo now houses a wide range of mammals. *Paldiski mnt 145 • 694 3300 • Open 9am–7pm May–Aug; 9am–5pm Mar, Apr, Sep & Oct; 9am–3pm Nov–Feb • Adm • www.tallinnzoo.ee*

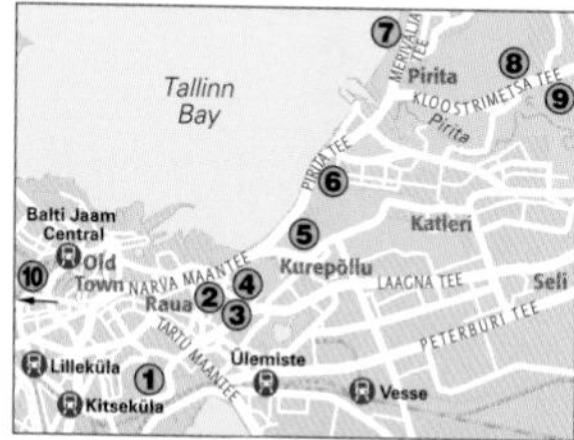

Price Categories

For a three course meal for one with half a bottle of wine (or equivalent meal), taxes and extra charges.

€	under €15
€€	€15–€25
€€€	€25–€35
€€€€	€35–€50
€€€€€	over €50

Left **KUMU Café**

TOP 10 Cafés and Restaurants

1 Botanical Gardens Café
This café in the Botanical Gardens' palm house is little more than a counter with a fridge full of soft drinks and a coffee machine, but the location can't be bettered *(see p99)*.

2 Cantina Carramba
Enjoy spicy Mexican-themed food at this colourful restaurant, though there are also plenty of steaks and grilled salmon dishes on offer. *Weizenbergi 20a • Map C5 • 601 3431 • Open noon–11pm Mon–Sat, noon–8pm Sun • €€€€*

3 Kadriorg Palace Café
Located on the ground floor of the Art Museum, this is an informal order-at-the-counter café with a tempting range of savoury pastries, dainty cakes and chocolates. *Weizenbergi 37 • Map C5 • Open 10am–5pm Tue–Sun*

4 KUMU Café
The KUMU café has soups, quiches and cakes on its menu and is an ideal spot to take a post-gallery breather. *Weizenbergi 34 • Map C5 • Open 11am–6pm Mon, 11am–7pm Tue–Sun • €€*

5 NOP Café
Occupying a wooden house in a quaint residential street, this combined organic food store and café is a big hit with health-conscious locals. The food is top-notch. *Köleri 1 • Map B5 • 603 2270 • Tram no. 1 or no. 3 • Open 8am–8pm • €€*

6 Park Café
Situated at the western entrance to Kadriorg Park, this café offers pastries, cakes and handmade chocolates served by waitresses in frilly aprons. *Weizenbergi 22 • Map C5 • 601 3040 • Open 10am–8pm Tue–Sun • €€*

7 Kolu Kõrts Tavern
Try rural Estonian dishes such as *hernesupp* (yellow pea soup), *mulgipuder* (mashed up potato and barley) and *karbonaad* (fatty pork chop) at this traditional tavern *(see p30)*.

8 Restoran & Spaghetteria Kadriorg
This chic restaurant serves up homemade pasta, risottos and steak and fish dishes. *Weizenbergi 18 • Map C5 • 601 3636 • Tram no. 1 or no. 3 • Open noon–11pm Mon–Sat, 1–5pm Sun • €€€€*

9 Winners Sports Lounge
Right beside the Pirita bridge, this pub has a sporty theme, with pictures of footballers and Formula 1 drivers lining the walls. The menu is wide ranging. *Kloostri tee 6 • Map E3 • 601 4095 • Open 11:30am–midnight • €€€*

10 Villa Thai
A short walk west of Kadriorg, Villa Thai serves Thai and Indian dishes. There are plenty of vegetarian and seafood options, and an inexpensive lunchtime menu. *Vilmsi 6 • Map B5 • 641 9347 • Open noon–11pm • €€€*

Olde Hansa

STREETSMART

Left **Outdoor eating in the summer, Town Hall Square** Right **Tallinn airport**

Top 10 Planning Your Trip

1 When to Go

Tallinn is an enjoyable destination whatever the time of year. Spring and summer see the most sunshine, and the outdoor tables of cafés and restaurants bring vivacity to the streets. Daylight lasts longest in mid-to-late June, when blue skies can be enjoyed until 11pm or later. Winter can also be a delightful time to visit, with snow cover remaining on the ground for weeks on end – although bear in mind that from December to March the average daily temperature remains well below zero.

2 Peak Seasons

July and August are the busiest months and hotel prices are at their highest during this period. Easter and the weeks leading up to Christmas are also increasingly popular. The main annual holiday for the Estonians themselves is 24 June (Midsummer Day) – when many locals head out of town for a long weekend, leaving central Tallinn comparatively deserted.

3 What to Pack

Even at the height of summer you will encounter cool evenings and occasional rain, so pullovers, waterproof jackets and compact umbrellas are essential. You should also bring practical footwear for city sightseeing – many of Tallinn's streets have retained their 19th-century cobblestones. In winter you will need lots of layers and warm head covering to withstand the extreme cold.

4 Passports and Visas

Citizens of the EU can enter Estonia without a visa and stay for as long as they like, although they should register with the police after 90 days. Citizens of the USA, Canada, Australia and New Zealand can visit visa-free for 90 days. Citizens of other countries should contact their local Estonian consulate to check current regulations.

5 Travel Insurance

Although the Estonian health care system has reciprocal agreements with EU and a number of other foreign countries, it is still a good idea to take out insurance cover for health problems, trip cancellation, flight delay and lost luggage.

6 Airlines

National airline Estonian Air flies to Tallinn from several European capitals including London, Paris, Rome and Stockholm. Both Finnair and Latvian carrier Air Baltic offer one-stop flights to Tallinn via Helsinki and Riga respectively. Low-cost airline easyJet flies to Tallinn from the London Stansted airport as well as Liverpool.

7 Customs

Visitors arriving from the EU are allowed to bring up to 800 cigarettes, 10 litres of spirits and 90 litres of wine. Arrivals from outside the EU can bring 40 cigarettes, one litre of spirits and two litres of wine.

8 Electricity

The Estonian electricity supply is 220v and standard continental 2-pronged plugs are required. Visitors from the UK and North America will need an adaptor, available at most airports.

9 Maps

The most up-to-date maps of Tallinn are produced by Estonian publisher Regio. They can be bought in bookshops in Tallinn, or from specialist bookshops outside the country.

10 Time Zone

Tallinn is in the East European time zone and is two hours ahead of the UK, seven hours ahead of US Eastern Standard Time and ten hours behind Australian Eastern Standard Time.

Preceding pages **Street sign, Olde Hansa**

Left **The Tallink ferry** Centre **Cycling at Pirita Tee** Right **Baalti Jaam train station**

TOP 10 Getting There and Around

1 By Air
Tallinn is served by direct flights from several European cities. If travelling from outside Europe, a one-stop or two-stop flight is required. Flights from London take 3hrs.

2 Tallinn Airport
The airport is 4km (2.5 miles) east of the city centre in Ülemiste, and has an exchange counter, an ATM and car hire desks. It is linked to the centre every 20–30 minutes by bus no. 2. A taxi to the centre costs around €10. *605 8888 • www.tallinn-airport.ee*

3 By Train
Moscow is the only major foreign city linked to Tallinn by rail. Trains arrive at the Balti Jaam station, which is an easily walkable half a km west of the Old Town. *631 0044 • www.gorail.ee*

4 By Bus
There are international buses from St Petersburg, Riga and Vilnius to Tallinn. The bus station is 2 km (1.25 miles) east of the centre. Trams no. 2 and 4 will take you from here to Viru väljak outside the Old Town. *12550 • www.bussireisid.ee*

5 By Car
Tallinn is 315 km (197 miles) from Riga, Latvia's capital and 525 km (326 miles) from the Lithuanian capital Vilnius, making it easy to drive here as part of a general Baltic tour. Driving here from Western Europe, however, could take one or two days. With regular car ferries from Helsinki and Stockholm, driving to Tallinn from Scandinavia is also possible. *ABC Autorent 674 7781 Budget 605 8600 • www.budget.ee; www.abcrent.ee*

6 By Boat
There are regular catamarans and car ferries to Tallinn from the Finnish capital Helsinki, 90 km (56 miles) north across the Baltic Sea. Lindaline operates passenger-only catamarans from May to October; while Tallink, Viking and Eckerö operate car ferries all year round. Tallink also operates a daily ferry to Tallinn from Stockholm, which takes 16 hours. *Lindaline 699 9333; Tallink 640 9808; Eckerö 664 6000; Viking 666 3966 • www.lindaliini.ee; www.tallinksilja.com; www.eckeroline.ee; www.vikingline.fi*

7 Public Transport in Tallinn
Tallinn has a comprehensive network of buses and trams. Single-journey tickets cost €1 in advance from newspaper kiosks, or €1.60 from the driver. You can also buy a book of ten tickets (€8), or a 72-hour ticket (€6) from the kiosks.

8 Cycling
Cycling may be a bumpy way of touring the cobbled streets of the Old Town but it's a great means of travelling to suburban sites like Kadriorg Park or Pirita Beach. Various outfits rent out bicycles. City Bike is one of the biggest, and also organizes tours of Tallinn's historical sites. Bicycle hire rates start at around €2.60 per hour, €13 per day. *City Bike Uus 33 • 511 1819 • www.citybike.ee*

9 Taxis
Taxis can be found at all major intersections leading to the Old Town. Fares are displayed on a sticker in the taxi window – study these before getting in. Standard fares should be around €3.50 initial charge, followed by €0.80 per km (€1 per km between 8pm-6am). The best way to ensure fair rates is to book by phone from a reputable firm such as Tallink taxi or Tulika, which also accept card payment. *Tallink: 640 8921; Tulika: 612 0001*

10 Walking
Tallinn is a small capital city and its Old Town is pedestrianized, making it the perfect place to explore on foot. The port area northeast of the Old Town and the Kalamaja district to the northwest are also ideal for strolling.

The Tallinn Card entitles holders to free use of public transport **see p106.**

Left **Traveller info tent** Centre **Tourist Information Office sign** Right **Tallinn Card**

Top 10 Useful Information

1 Tourist Information

Tallinn's main tourist office is in the centre of the Old Town, with a subsidiary office in the Viru keskus shopping centre. Both are helpful and provide free maps to the city. *Niguliste 2 • Map J4 • 645 7777 • Open 9am–6pm Mon–Fri, 10am–5pm Sat & Sun • www.tourism.tallinn.ee*

2 Traveller Info Tent

Set up by students in the park opposite the tourist office, the Traveller Info Tent provides information for younger travellers and organizes offbeat walking and cycling tours of the city. They also provide listings of rock concerts and club nights. *Niguliste • Map J4 • 5554 2111 • Open 9am–7pm Jun–Aug • www.traveller.ee*

3 The Tallinn Card

Sold at the tourist office, the Tallinn card provides free entry to most museums and galleries, free use of public transport, free bike hire, a free city tour, and discounts in some restaurants. The card costs €12 (€6 for children up to 14) for 6 hours; €24 (€13) for 24 hours; €32 (€15) for 48 hours; and €40 (€16) for 72 hours. *www.tallinncard.ee*

4 Opening Hours

Many restaurants, sights and museums in Tallinn keep rather erratic hours, and almost all open longer in summer than in winter. Opening hours are generally more regular in the summer, but most museums are shut on Mondays. It is prudent to phone ahead for opening times.

5 Tallinn In Your Pocket

This bi-monthly English-language visitors' guide offers write-ups and reviews of restaurants, hotels and businesses. *www.inyourpocket.com*

6 The Baltic Times

This weekly English newspaper covers events in Lithuania, Latvia and Estonia. It frequently carries coverage of Tallinn's restaurant, bar and cultural scene.

7 Toilets

All restaurants and cafés have toilets for customers. Public toilets are located on Lossi plats, Toompea and Viru. Toilets for men are marked by the letter "M" or a triangle symbol pointing downwards; toilets for women are marked by the letter "N" or a triangle symbol pointing upwards.

8 Language

Estonian is a member of the Finno-Ugric family of languages, and is related to Finnish and – more distantly – to Hungarian. Estonians educated after the restoration of independence in 1991 have good knowledge of English. However, over 30% of the population count Russian as their mother tongue and it is often heard on the streets.

9 Disabled Travellers

The cobbled streets of the Old Town and Toompea are difficult terrain for wheelchair users. Major museums and galleries are equipped with ramps and lifts. Most hotels of three star rating and above have rooms equipped for disabled travellers.

10 Gay and Lesbian Travellers

Tallinn is a relatively open city although conservative attitudes prevail among certain sections of the public. There are a few openly gay clubs in the city.

Public Holidays

- *1 January*
- *24 February (Independence Day)*
- *Good Friday*
- *Easter Sunday*
- *1 May*
- *23 June (Victory Day; the anniversary of 1919's Battle of Cesis)*
- *24 June (St John's Day)*
- *20 August (Restoration of Independence)*
- *Christmas Eve*
- *Christmas Day*
- *Boxing Day*

Left **High heels on cobblestones** Centre **Crime warning sign** Right **Bus and tram tickets**

TOP 10 Things to Avoid

1 Pickpockets

The main operating areas for pickpockets are open-air markets, crowded trams and buses and busy city-centre bars that are frequented by foreigners. Keep your belongings closely guarded and don't leave them unattended or set them down on a bench.

2 Bureaux de Change

Not all of Tallinn's bureaux de change are rip-offs by any means, but many of the establishments lining the Old Town's principal streets offer miserable exchange rates to gullible newcomers. Shop around to find the best rate or go to a bank.

3 Drinking in the Street

Unless you are on a designated restaurant or bar terrace, drinking alcohol on the street is illegal and punishable by a fine. Police do, however, turn a blind eye to outdoor drinking in a handful of locations that are popular with local youth – notably Roheline turg on Pikk, and Harjumägi hill.

4 Not Packing Enough Warm Clothes

Winter can be extremely harsh, with temperatures staying below 0°C for weeks or indeed months on end. Warm clothes and some form of head covering are vital if you want to roam the streets in comfort. Summer too can be unpredictable, with sunny days frequently followed by chilly or rainy nights – so don't forget to pack pullovers, jackets and an umbrella.

5 Failing to Punch Your Tram Ticket

Tickets for buses, trolleybuses and trams need to be validated by punching them in the machines near the entrances. Failure to do this will leave you with an invalid ticket – and if an inspector happens to catch you, an on-the-spot fine of €40.

6 Travelling in Overpriced Taxis

Most taxis in Tallinn are operated by reputable companies and have rates per kilometre clearly marked in the window. However visitors should be on the lookout for taxis – frequently parked at key entrances to the Old Town – that display no prices at all, or prices in illegible print. Step into one of these and you could end up paying a lot more than you bargained for.

7 Touring the Old Town in High-Heeled Shoes

Tallinn's cobbled alley-ways are hardly ideal for high-heeled shoes which can turn a half-day sightseeing into an awkward, energy-sapping process. In winter the problem can be compounded by snow and ice. Practical shoes with a tread are better suited to the terrain.

8 Stag Parties

Tallinn is by no means as overrun by stag parties as some other European capitals. However, certain parts of the Old Town can be thick with groups of males on Friday and Saturday nights. At these times, the popular strip of bars and pubs along Suur-kaarja is probably best left to them.

9 Women Offering Company to Lone Males

Approaches from over-friendly women in bars or on the streets are common. Their main objective is to lure you to a bar with expensive drinks and bouncers you can't argue with.

10 Offers of Free Entry to Strip Clubs

Visitors to Tallinn will frequently be approached by touts offering free entry to sex clubs or a reduced-price round of drinks. However attractive these offers may look, you will be hit with an extortionate bar bill sooner or later.

Left **Exchange sign** Centre **People posting postcards** Right **ATM machine**

Top 10 Banking and Communications

1 Money

Estonia adopted the euro on 1 January 2011. Coins come in denominations of 1, 2, 5, 10 and 50 cents, and €1 and €2; while notes in circulation are €5, €10, €20, €50, €100, €200 and €500.

2 Banks

Most banks are open 9am–6pm from Monday to Friday, and 10am–3pm on Saturdays. Major high-street banks include Nordea, SEB and Swedbank. They usually offer better rates than exchange bureaux, but the queues are longer.

3 Changing Money

There are exchange bureaux throughout the city centre, although those on the tourist-trodden routes of the Old Town (notably along Viru and around Town Hall Square) do not offer the best rates. Examine the rates in the window before committing yourself. One exchange bureau that offers decent rates and has long opening hours is Tavid on Aia. *Aia 5 • Open 24hr*

4 ATMs

The easiest way to obtain local currency is with a credit or debit card from ATMs, which are found throughout the city and have instructions in Estonian, Russian and English. A transaction fee will be charged by the card issuer, but the exchange rate will be reasonably close to the official rate offered by the main banks.

5 Credit Cards and Traveller's Cheques

Credit and debit cards are now almost universally accepted in Tallinn. Traveller's cheques can be exchanged at banks, although this can often be a time-consuming procedure and may involve a high commission fee.

6 Telephones

Almost all Tallinn residents carry mobile phones. Estonian mobile phone operators EMT, Elisa and Tele2 offer pre-paid SIM cards that allow you to make local calls at local rates. Check if your mobile phone can be used with local SIM cards issued by various operators, or it may lock when you insert one. In 2011, the world's first Skype phone booth opened in Lennart Meri Tallinn Airport, allowing travellers with Skype accounts to make free video calls. More such booths are planned throughout the country.

7 Post

Tallinn's main post office is located just outside the Old Town on Narva mnt. The branch post office on Viru is a good place to buy stamps and send postcards, but does not offer services such as sending parcels. *Narva mnt. 1 (Central Post Office); Map L3; Open 8am–8pm Mon–Fri, 9am–5pm Sat • Old Town: Viru 20; Map K4; Open 10am–6pm Mon–Fri*

8 Internet

Estonia is among the most Internet-conscious countries in Europe and free Wi-Fi coverage is available in almost all hotels, restaurants and cafés. There aren't many Internet cafés but most hostels and hotels will have at least one computer terminal that guests can use.

9 Newspapers and Magazines

A small selection of English-language newspapers are available from kiosks in central Tallinn. They usually arrive a day after publication. International fashion and lifestyle magazines are available from news-agents and bookshops.

10 Television

Most hotel rooms have televisions offering a number of cable or satellite channels, with international news channels such as BBC, CNN or EuroNews included. The national television broadcasts a large number of English-language films, in the original language with Estonian subtitles.

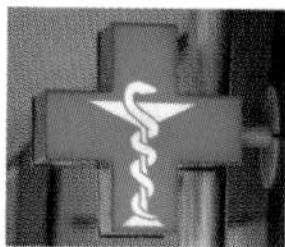

Left **Pharmacy sign** Centre **Police car** Right **No smoking sign**

Top 10 Security and Health

1 Emergency Numbers
The number for fire, police and ambulance is 112 and the operators speak English. For non-urgent health problems, ring Tallinn's first-aid hotline 697 1145 for advice on which hospital or clinic specializes in treating your ailment.

2 Police
The Estonian word for police is *politsei*. Most police officers speak English and are happy to help tourists with directions. You are legally obliged to carry some form of identification with you at all times.

3 Hospitals
Tallinn's hospitals are excellent and foreigners will be given free medical care in an emergency, but you should always take out travel insurance as a precaution. *Tallinn General Hospital Ravi 18 • 622 7070 • www.itk.ee*

4 Dentists
Estonian dental treatment is good and relatively cheap. Tallinna Hambapolikliinik is the city's biggest dental clinic while Terve Hammas is a private practice with English-speaking staff. *Tallinna Hambapolikliinik: Toompuiestee 4; Terve Hammas: Faehlmanni 5 • Tallinna Hambapolikliinik: 611 9230; Terve Hammas: 646 1493 • www.hambapol.ee; www.tervehammas.ee*

5 Pharmacies and Opticians
The Estonian word for pharmacy is *apteek*. Internationally manufactured drugs are widely available in Estonia. Most pharmacies are open from 9am–7 or 8pm Mon–Fri, 10am–5 or 6pm on Saturdays and Sundays. Tõnismäe apteek is a centrally-located pharmacy that has an emergency counter open 24 hours. If you run out of contact lenses, cleaning fluids or other supplies then head for an optician with weekend opening hours such as Lens Optika. *Tõnismäe apteek: Tõnismägi 5; Lens Optika: Foorum shopping centre, Narva mnt 5; Tõnismäe apteek: 644 2282; Lens Optika: 664 0404*

6 Crime
There is very little violent crime in Tallinn. Most problems arise from petty theft in crowded areas frequented by foreigners. Tallinn can be a rowdy place on Friday nights with revellers touring the local bars, although the resulting noisy behaviour is mostly good-natured and unthreatening.

7 Precautions
Avoiding petty thieves and pickpockets in Tallinn is mostly a question of common sense. Handbags and rucksacks should be securely fastened and held close to the body. Avoid flashing large sums of money in public, and don't keep expensive cameras and mobile phones on restaurant and café tables. Also, don't leave coats or bags draped over seats when in crowded bars.

8 Consulates
Most major countries have embassies or consulates in Tallinn. In an emergency, especially if you have any dealings with the police, insist that they immediately contact your consulate.

9 Smoking
Smoking is banned in enclosed public spaces except for bars or clubs that have a designated smoking area. Smoking is allowed on the outdoor terraces of restaurants, cafés and bars.

10 Water
Tapwater in Tallinn is safe to drink, and whether or not you prefer to buy bottled water is really a matter of taste.

Consulates
Canada • Tomkooli 13 • Map H3 • 627 3311 • Tallinn@canada.ee

UK • Wismari 6 • Map G5 • 667 4700 • www.britishembassy.ee

USA • Kentmanni 20 • Map K5 • 668 8100 • www.usemb.ee

Left **Café Kehrwieder** Centre **Pirukas** Right **Diners at Olde Hansa restaurant**

TOP 10 Dining Tips

1 Vegetarians

Tallinn has few vegetarian restaurants. Most vegetarians will have to make do with a combination of salads and side orders, although restaurants serving Indian or Far Eastern cuisine invariably offer vegetarian dishes. Italian restaurants are a good place to seek out meat-free pastas.

2 Reservations

Most restaurants in Tallinn have a fast turn-over and it's often possible to find a seat immediately or after waiting for a few minutes. However, if you are planning to dine at a highly reputed restaurant, do reserve a table in advance, especially on weekends.

3 Ordering

In restaurants and formal or stylish cafés, table service is the norm. However, in bars and unpretentious cafés patronized by locals, it is more common to order your food at the counter and pay for it beforehand.

4 Paying

Estonian waitstaff don't automatically come to your table just because your plate is empty and you may well have to summon their attention in order to request the bill. Credit cards are accepted almost everywhere.

5 Tipping

It is common to add 10% to the bill, although most people simply round up to the nearest figure.

6 Smoking

Smoking is banned in all restaurants and cafés. Some bars have a designated smoking area, but this may be no more than a cramped cubicle. Restaurants and cafés usually allow smoking on the outdoor terrace in summer and some outdoor tables may be set aside for non-smokers.

7 Breakfast

Even the cheapest hotel will include a continental breakfast in the room tarriff. Most hotels with three stars or above offer a buffet breakfast, featuring traditional Estonian food (porridge, marinated fish and occasionally blood sausage) alongside cereals and scrambled eggs. Cafés in central Tallinn rarely offer breakfast. You can visit Kehrwieder *(see p52)* on Town Hall Square for an early morning coffee and a pastry, while the Elsebet bakery has a sit-down section where you can enjoy freshly baked goods.

Elsebet bakery: Viru 2; 646 6995; Open 8am–5pm Mon–Sat, 9am–5pm Sun

8 Late-Night Dining

Most restaurant kitchens shut by around 11pm in Tallinn, although some establishments such as the bar-restaurant Clazz *(see p61)* continue serving meals after midnight. Hesburger serves up burgers and fries until 5am on Saturdays, while Taco Express in the Old Town is open 24 hours on weekends.

Hesburger: Viru 27a; Open 9am–11pm Mon–Fri, 9am–5am Sat • Taco Express: Suur-karja 18; Open 9am–7pm Mon–Fri, 11am–10am Sat & Sun

9 Fast Food

Pirukas, the archetypal Estonian fast food, is a bite-sized pastry with savoury fillings. Almost every café in the Old Town will have a selection displayed on the counter. The best place for a quick sit-down meal is Lido *(see p93)*, a Latvian self-service chain that offers hearty portions of meat, fish and potato dishes in a folksy interior.

10 Ethnic Food

Non-European food is easy to find in Tallinn, with several established Chinese and Indian eateries now joined by Japanese, Middle Eastern and Thai options. The biggest international influence on Tallinn's dining scene comes from the Caucasus – the skewer-grilled shashlik *(saslöök)* is a regular feature of most local restaurants and fast food stalls.

Left **Knitwear at Müürivahe Market** Centre **Solaris shopping centre** Right **Souvenirs**

Top 10 Shopping Tips

1 Credit Cards

Credit and debit cards are popular among Estonians, who tend to use plastic to pay for the smallest of purchases. As a result credit cards are accepted everywhere in Tallinn except for small shops in the suburbs. A sign on the shop window usually indicates which cards are accepted.

2 VAT Refunds

Non-EU residents are entitled to a VAT refund on all goods bought in Estonia. Ask for a Fiscal Receipt and a VAT reclaim form – these act as export and tax refund documents for your purchases. Present these at a tax refund office at the airport or a land border, with the goods purchased, to collect your VAT refund. A service charge of around 10% is deducted when the refund is calculated.

3 Opening Hours

Shops in Tallinn are usually open 9/10am–7/8pm Monday to Friday, and 10am–5pm on Saturday. Many souvenir outlets in the Old Town are also open 10am–5pm on a Sunday.

4 Traditional Crafts

Head to Tallinn's Old Town to seek out traditional items such as wooden utensils, ceramics and iron-mongery. Established craft shops *(see p58)* offer a great choice of authentic items. Street stalls and glitzy souvenir shops frequently stock items which are mass-produced elsewhere.

5 Traditional Clothing

Estonia is famous for its handmade patterned woollens, felt hats, and linen ware made by local craftspeople. There is a daily market selling woolly jumpers and socks on Müürivahe *(see p59)*. Elsewhere, however, avoid street sellers and head for handicraft outlets such as Katariina Gild *(see p58)*, Eesti käsitöö and Hindrikus *(see p84)*.

6 Department Stores and Shopping Centres

Tallinn's best department store is the Finnish chain Stockmann, which sells everything from food to domestic appliances. There are several shopping centres where you will find international-brand shops plus plenty of cafés – both Viru Keskus and Solaris are located conveniently near the centre.

7 Modern Designs

Tallinn is a great place to seek out contemporary clothes and domestic items produced by local designers. Nu Nordic is a good place to buy fashion accessories and unusual gifts, while Bogapott *(see p84)* is the best place to shop for designer jewellery, ceramics and graphic art.

8 Markets

Tallinn's most colourful food market is the Central Market *(see p59)* near the bus station. An organic food market takes place in the central plaza of the Rotermann quarter daily, augmented by an arts-and-crafts section at weekends. Seafood delicacies and smoked eel are sold at the fish market held on Kalaranna every Saturday.

9 Buying Food and Drink

Central places to pick up food-and-drink supplies include the Rimi supermarket on Aia, and the supermarket in the basement of the Viru Keskus shopping centre. These and a number of central outlets sell a wide range of drinks – however, do remember that the sale of alcoholic drinks from shops is illegal from 10pm to 10am.

10 Books

International magazines, English-language novels and lavishly illustrated books about Estonian land and culture can be bought from the Rahva Raamat bookstore *(see p84)*, conveniently located near the Old Town.

Left **Schlössle hotel** Right **Barons hotel** Right **St Petersbourg hotel**

TOP 10 Luxury Hotels

1 Barons

Enjoying a good Old Town location, Barons occupies a former bank building that preserves much of its Art Nouveau-era decoration, including an old-style cage lift in the lobby. Standard rooms are smart and chic, while deluxe rooms have their own private sauna. *Suur-Karja 7 • Map J4 • 699 9700 • www.baronshotel.ee • €€€*

2 My City Hotel

Housed in a handsome 18th-century building in the Old Town, My City Hotel provides plush rooms decorated in rich reds, browns and ochre. The sauna and Jacuzzi room is the perfect place to relax. *Vana-Posti 11/13 • Map J4 • 622 0900 • www.mycityhotel.ee • €€€*

3 Merchants House

This beautifully renovated 14th-century building presents a mixture of Gothic and contemporary styles. The rooms are luxurious and the hotel's labyrinthine corridors and stairways provide a sense of medieval adventure. Guests can use the basement sauna. *Dunkri 4/6 • Map J3 • 697 7500 • www.merchantshousehotel.com • €€€*

4 Meriton Old Town Garden

Occupying a historic mansion with a charming garden in the courtyard, this hotel enjoys a prime location on one of the Old Town's prettiest streets. The "economy" rooms are quite small so opt for a "standard" double if you want to spread yourself out. *Pikk 29/Lai 24 • Map J4 • 667 7111 • www.meritonhotels.com • €€€*

5 Radisson Blu Hotel Tallinn

This immaculately run hotel in a sleek 24-floor tower offers rooms with quirky design touches, many coming with great views of the city. Sauna, gym and penthouse café-bar are among the extras. *Rävala pst 3 • Map L5 • 682 3000 • www.tallinn.radissonblu.com • €€€*

6 St Petersbourg

The oldest continually functioning hotel in the city, St Petersbourg is just round the corner from the Town Hall Square. The rooms are furnished in warm colours, while the lobby boasts a mixture of 19th-century and Art Deco styles. *Rataskaevu 7 • Map H3 • 628 6500 • www.hotelstpetersbourg.com • €€€*

7 Savoy Boutique

Located in a 20th-century office block that once served as the Estonian Ministry of Culture, the Savoy boasts a central location, well-equipped rooms and attentive staff. Art Deco design touches and prints by Estonian artists add to the refined air. *Suur-Karja 17/19 • Map J4 • 680 6688 • www.tallinnhotels.ee • €€€€*

8 Schlössle

Comprising three medieval buildings knocked into one, the five-star Schlössle offers bright rooms in creamy colours, some with timber ceiling beams. Courtyard-facing rooms are far quieter than those facing the street. *Pühavaimu 13/15 • Map J3 • 699 7700 • www.schloesslehotel.com • €€€€*

9 Swissotel

This black monolith rising above the city's main business district offers chic modern rooms with hardwood floors, designer fabrics and bedside coffee-making machines. An inviting swimming pool and spa centre takes up a whole floor. *Tornimäe 3 • Map M5 • 624 0000 • www.tallinn.swissotel.com • €€€€*

10 Three Sisters

Tallinn's premier boutique hotel occupies a trio of magnificently converted medieval houses. The interior boasts spiral staircases, a library with a fireplace and a wine cellar. All rooms come with flat-screen TVs. *Pikk 71/Tolli 2 • Map K2 • 630 6300 • www.threesistershotel.com • €€€€€*

Always check in advance of booking whether your hotel has air conditioning if you are planning a summer visit.

Left **Wellness centre, Kalev Spa hotel**

Price Categories

For a standard, double room per night (with breakfast if included), taxes and extra charges.		
	€	under €50
	€€	€50–100
	€€€	€100–150
	€€€€	€150–200
	€€€€€	over €200

TOP 10 Mid-Range Hotels

1 Braavo

With accommodation units arranged around the car park of a popular health club and gym, Braavo is informal, friendly and excellent value. Rooms are simple but bright and the Old Town is a mere two-minute walk across the street. *Aia 2 • Map K2 • 699 9777 • www.braavo.ee • €€*

2 Park Inn

A large hotel diagonally opposite the Viru Keskus shopping centre, the Park Inn is only a short hop from the Old Town and offers well-equipped rooms at a middle-market price. The slightly more expensive business rooms and family rooms come with electric kettles. *Narva mnt 7c • Map M3 • 669 0690 • www.parkinn.com • €€*

3 Domina Inn Ilmarine

This stylish conversion of a red-brick factory building provides smart and spacious rooms on the fringe of the Kalamaja district, a ten-minute walk from the Old Town. There is a sauna and beauty salon on the premises. *Põhja pst. 23 • Map J1 • 614 0900 • www.dominahotels.com • €€*

4 Kalev Spa

The centrally located Kalev Spa offers rooms right next to a large swimming-pool complex. Rooms are decorated in warm colours and a wide range of massages and beauty treatments are available in the hotel's spa centre. *Aia 18 • Map K2 • 649 3300 • www.kalevspa.ee • €€*

5 Meriton Old Town

The Meriton is housed in a characterful 19th-century building that backs onto parts of the city fortifications, which accounts for the curving walls in the reception area. Rooms have a warm, cosy ambience and the social areas are bright and welcoming. *Lai 49 • Map J2 • 614 1300 • www.meritonhotels.com • €€€*

6 Metropol

Situated in the middle of the atmospheric Rotermann Quarter, only a short walk from the Old Town, the Metropol is a modern building with a wealth of on-site facilities – sauna, massage centre and beauty salon included. Rooms are plain but comfortable. *Roseni 13 • Map L3 • 667 4500 • www.metropol.ee • €€*

7 Kreutzwald Hotel Tallinn

Excellent value for money and only a short walk from the Old Town, the Kreutzwald Hotel offers smart rooms each of which come with computer terminals and tea- and coffee-making facilities. There is a sauna and gym on the premises. *Endla 23 • Map A5 • 666 4800 • www.uniquestay.com • €€€*

8 Old Town Maestro's

Occupying a tall 15th-century house in the heart of the Old Town nightlife district, Maestro's offers classy and quite spacious rooms decked out in earthy matt colours. Bathrooms benefit from underfloor heating and there is also a sauna on site. *Suur-Karja 10 • Map J4 • 626 2000 • www.maestrohotel.ee • €€*

9 St Barbara

An attractive 19th-century stone building is the scene for this medium-sized hotel just off Vabaduse väljak, an ideal location for sightseeing. The en suite rooms are decorated in subdued relaxing colours. Family rooms come with extra beds for children. *Roosikrantsi 2a • Map J5 • 640 0040 • www.stbarbara.ee • €€*

10 Sokos Hotel Viru

A 500-room establishment built by Finns in the 1970s, the Viru was considered the top hotel in the Soviet Union at the time, and it still maintains high standards. Rooms are decorated in warm colours and there are good views from the upper floors. *Viru väljak 4 • Map L4 • 680 9300 • www.viru.ee • €€€*

Recommend your favourite hotel on **traveldk.com**

Left **Erel apartments** Centre **Villa Hortensia** Right **Old House Guesthouse**

Top 10 Apartments, Rentals and B&Bs

1 Apartment 24

This agency offers fully equipped apartments in central locations, many of them in atmospheric corners of the Old Town. All apartments are self-catering with TV; some come with additional facilities such as washing machines and saunas. *Narva 5-1 • Map L3 • 5568 5351 • www.apartment24.ee • €50–€70*

2 City Style Apartments

City Style rent out a variety of holiday apart-ments, ranging from two-person studios to three-bedroom family apartments. Most properties are located in the Old Town or are an easy walk from it. All apartments feature well-equipped kitchens, some come with cable TV. *Gonsiori 3 • Map M4 • 5303 8522 • www.citystyle-apartments.ee • €35–€150*

3 Erel

Erel offers smart accommodation in serviced two-bedroom apartments either in the Old Town or just outside it. They also have a big choice of comfortable one- to three-bedroom flats throughout the Old Town. *Paldiski mnt. 26A • 663 1640 • www.erel.ee • €69–€249*

4 Ites

The Ites has accommodation ranging from cosy studios to three-bedroom flats, many with charming Old Town locations. All have a fully equipped kitchen, most also have a washing machine and cable TV. Ites also arranges car hire. *Harju 6 • Map H5 • 631 0637 • www.ites.ee • €80–€130*

5 Old House Guesthouse

A good-value bed-and-breakfast in the Old Town offering a handful of small but attractive rooms with shared toilet and bathroom facilities in the hallway. The owners also rent out 2- to 4-person apartments in the Old Town. *Uus 22 • Map K2 • 641 1464 • www.oldhouse.ee • €*

6 Pilve Apartment Hotel

This modern development in residential streets 1km (half a mile) south of the Old Town offers smart apartments ranging in size from 2-person studios to 3-bedroom family dwellings. Breakfast can be delivered to your apartment for a few extra euros. *Pilve 4 • Map A5 • 504 5444 • www.apartment.ee • €35–€190*

7 Poska Villa

Offering five bright and cheerful rooms, this charming B&B occupies a historic timber-built house in leafy suburban streets near Kadriorg Park. The cosy top-floor rooms come with sloping attic ceilings. Profits from the business go towards a senior citizens' charity. *Poska 15 • Map C5 • 601 3601 • www.hot.ee/poskavilla • €42–€63*

8 Sakala Residence

The Sakala Residence offers a range of swish one- to three-bedroom apartments, all located in a renovated block just behind Solaris *(see p59)*. The apartments boast superb modern kitchens, and provisions can be ordered in advance. *Sakala 16 • Map J5 • 663 1640 • www.sakalaresidence.ee • €70–€236*

9 Valge Villa

This suburban B&B in the calm Kristiine district, southwest of the Old Town, offers a handful of cosy doubles, as well as three- to four-person suites, all equipped with tea- and coffee-making facilities. The home-cooked breakfast is a major plus. *Kännu 26/2 • 654 2302 • www.white-villa.com • €35–€50*

10 Villa Hortensia

Located in the Masters' Courtyard, this guesthouse squeezes six en suite rooms into an atmospheric medieval building with exposed stonework and steep attic ceilings. Breakfast isn't included but there are plenty of cafés nearby. *Vene 6 • Map J3 • 504 6113 • www.hoov.ee • €50*

Price Categories

For a standard, double room per night (with breakfast if included), taxes and extra charges.	
€	under €50
€€	€50–€100
€€€	€100–€150
€€€€	€150–€200
€€€€€	over €200

Left **Common room, Tallinn Backpackers** Right **Euphoria Hostel**

Top 10 Budget Stays

1 Euphoria Hostel
Just round the corner from Vabaduse väljak, Euphoria offers neat dorms, self-contained doubles and a small kitchen. Draped with oriental textiles, the relaxing common room features a range of musical instruments. *Roosikrantsi 4 • Map J5 • 5837 3602 • http://euphoria.traveller.ee • €*

2 G9
Situated on the third floor of an office building a short walk away from the Old Town, G9 offers decent rooms at good rates. Breakfast in the nearby Café Narva costs a few extra euros. *Gonsiori 9 • Map M4 • 626 7130 • www.hotelg9.ee • €*

3 Old House Hostel
The well-located Old House Hostel has a good choice of rooms, with singles, doubles and triples as well as more economical dorm accommodation. The common room features near-antique furniture. *Uus 26 • Map K2 • 641 1281 • www.oldhouse.ee • €*

4 Rasastra Bed & Breakfast
Rasastra organizes accommodation in local family homes, where guests will get a self-contained bedroom and use of their host's bathroom. Despite the title, breakfast isn't always part of the deal – and if it is available, you'll have to pay extra. *661 6291 • www.bedbreakfast.ee • €*

5 Go Hotel Schnelli
This outwardly dour building next to the Balti Jaam railway station harbours attractive and cosy rooms, with wine reds and woody browns predominating the colour scheme. East-facing rooms come with great views of Toompea Hill. *Toompuiestee 37 • Map G3 • 631 0102 • www.gohotels.ee • €*

6 Tallinn Backpackers
A popular hostel offering dorm accommodation in a superbly located medieval building. Its spacious common room and themed party nights make this one of Tallinn's most sociable hostels. Private rooms at separate Old Town locations are also available. Advance booking is essential. *Olevimägi 11-1 • Map J2 • 644 0298 • www.tallinnbackpackers.com • €*

7 Flying Kiwi Backpackers' Hostel
Located on the third and fourth floors of an old apartment building in the Old Town, this friendly hostel incorporates multiple-bunk dorm rooms on one floor and private doubles and triples on the floor below. A guest kitchen and helpful staff make for a pleasant stay. *Nunne 1 • Map J3 • 5821 3292 • www.flyingkiwitallinn.com • €*

8 Tallink Express
The ideal place for those arriving or leaving by ferry, this modern port-side hotel offers sparsely decorated but bright en suite rooms, each with a small TV and work desk. The lobby areas offer relaxing corners in which to socialize. *Sadama 1 • Map L1 • 667 8700 • www.hotels.tallink.com • €€*

9 Tatari 53
A pleasant and comfortable hotel in Tallinn's main business and shopping district, Tatari 53 offers en suite rooms in relaxing shades of grey and brown. The Old Town is within walking distance. *Tatari 53 • Map J5 • 640 5150 • www.tatari53.ee • €€*

10 City Hotel Tallinn
Just west of the Old Town, this cheap-but-chic option offers smart en suite rooms and a relaxing sitting room-cum-library. The basic bed-and-breakfast price is great value. Guests who require daily room-cleaning or towel-changing services pay extra. *Paldiski mnt 3 • Map G4 • 660 0700 • www.uniquestay.com • €*

General Index

Acknowledgments

The Author

Jonathan Bousfield was born in the UK and has been travelling in Central & Eastern Europe for as long as he can remember. A student of East European history and languages, he has authored the *DK Eyewitness Guide to Bulgaria, Rough Guide to the Baltic States,* and co-authored the *Rough Guide to Poland and Bulgaria.*

Photographer James Tye
Additional Photography Demetrio Carrasco
Fact Checker Nat Singer

At DK INDIA
Managing Editor Aruna Ghose
Editorial Manager Sheeba Bhatnagar
Design Manager Kavita Saha
Project Editor Vatsala Srivastava
Project Designer Neha Dhingra
Assistant Cartographic Manager Suresh Kumar
Cartographer Hassan Mohammad
Senior Picture Research Coordinator Taiyaba Khatoon
DTP Coordinator Azeem Siddiqui
Indexer Andy Kulkarni

At DK LONDON
Publisher Douglas Amrine
List Managers Julie Oughton, Christine Stroyan
Design Manager Mabel Chan
Senior Editor Sadie Smith
Designer Tracy Smith
Senior Cartographic Editor Casper Morris
Picture Research Assistant Marta Bescos Sanchez
Sr. DTP Designer Jason Little
Production Controller Emma Sparks
Revisions Team Shruti Bahl, Imogen Corke, Shikha Kulkarni, Irja Luks, Nicola Malone, Preeti Singh

Picture Credits
Placement Key- a-above; b-below/bottom; c-centre; f-far; l-left; r-right; t-top.

Photography Permissions
Dorling Kindersley would like to thank the following for their assistance and kind permission to photograph at their establishments:

AHHAA Science Centre, Anneli Viik Café, Bogapott, Bonaparte Restaurant, Café Mademoiselle, Café VS, Dome Church (Cathedral of Saint Mary the Virgin), Church of St Simeon and the Prophetess Hanna, C'est La Vie Restaurant & Café, Chakra Restaurant, Chocolaterie Pierre, City Musuem, Clazz Restoran & Club, Club Hollywood, Club Privé, Drink Bar & Grill, Estonian History Museum, Estonian Open-Air Museum, Estonian State Puppet and Youth Theatre (NUKU), Fish & Wine Restaurant, Hell Hunt Café, Hindrikus, Hotel St Petersbourg, Kadriog Palace Art Musuem, Kalev Spa Hotel, Kalev Water Park, Kehrwieder, Korter, KUMU Modern Art Museum, Maiasmokk, Master's Courtyard, Museum of Applied Art and Design, Museum of Occupations, Museum Restaurant, Niguliste Church, Old House Hostel, Olde Hansa Restaurant, Orthodox Cathedral of Alexander Nevsky, Patarei Prison Museum, Schlössle Hotel, Stenhus Restaurant, Tallinn Zoo,

Town Hall Pharmacy, Villa Hortensia, Viru Hotel, Von Krahli Aed, Von Krahl Teater.
Works of art have been reproduced with the permission of the following copyright holders: Sculpture room Installation *Seagull* © Villu Jaanisoo 27tl.

The publisher would like to thank the following individuals, companies, and picture libraries for their kind permission to reproduce their photographs:

ALAMY IMAGES: eye35.com 94–95.

THE ART MUSEUM OF ESTONIA: 12tr, 24tc, 36cla, 36br; Kaido Haagen 22br; Arne Maasik 26c; *Port of Tallinn* (1853) Oil, Aleksei Petrovitš Bogoljubov 24tl; *Beauty Directed by Prudence* (1770) Oil, Angelica Kauffmann 24cla; *Soldier's Tale* (1877) Oil, Ilja Jefrimovits Repin 25cr; *The Imprecation of Lorelei by the Monks* (1887) Oil, Johann Köler 26br; *Surprise* (1840) Oil, Carl Timoleon von Neff 27cra; *Nudes and Landscapes* (Installation), Original wallpaper, Oil paintings, Water colors (2010): paintings displayed include (left to right) *Nude* (2010) Oil, *Seascape* (2009) Oil, *Landscape* (2009) Oil, Merike Estna 27clb; *Norwegian Landscape with Pine* (1908–1910) Oil, Konrad Mägi 28tl; *Swimming the Horses* (1925–1930) Oil, Paul Burman 28tc; *At the Window* (1935) Oil, Arnold Akberg 28tr; *Linda Carrying a Stone* (1915) Pastel, Oskar Kallis 28bl; *Portrait of Mother* (1863) Oil, Johann Köler 38tl; *Summer* (Two Nudes) Painting from Triptytheon "Spring, Summer, Autumn" (1935), Oil Adamson-Eric 38tc; *Estonian Woman* (1975) Oil, Tõnu Virve 38tr; *Lady with Child* (1926) Oil, Arnold Akberg 38ca; *Lake* (1918–1920) Oil, Konrad Mägi 39tl.

ESTONIAN FOLK ART AND CRAFT UNION: 54tr, 55tr.

FOCUS: Nordic Photos 49bl; Kalju Suur 35cla.

THE ESTONIAN OPEN-AIR MUSEUM: 30–31c.

PHOTOLIBRARY: Focus Database 18–19c, 54br; Peter Erik Forsberg 102–103; Yadid Levy 10–11c; Superstock Inc 66–67.

RADISSON BLU: 50b.

TALLINN PHILHARMONIC SOCIETY: 54tl, 55cla, 55br.

WIKIPEDIA, THE FREE ENCYCLOPEDIA: 34tl, 34tc, 34tr, 34br, 35tr, 35br.

All other images © Dorling Kindersley
For further information see: www.dkimages.com

Special Editions of DK Travel Guides

DK Travel Guides can be purchased in bulk quantities at discounted prices for use in promotions or as premiums. We are also able to offer special editions and personalized jackets, corporate imprints, and excerpts from all of our books, tailored specifically to meet your own needs.

To find out more, please contact:

(in the United States) **SpecialSales@dk.com**

(in the UK) **travelspecialsales@uk.dk.com**

(in Canada) DK Special Sales at **general@tourmaline.ca**

(in Australia) **business.development@pearson.com.au**

Phrase Book

Guidelines for Pronunciation

Alphabet

The Estonian alphabet consists of the following letters: a, b, d, e, f, g, h, i, j, k, l, m, n, o, p, r, s, š, z, ž, t, u, v, õ, ä, ö, ü. The letters c, q, x, y, z are used only in proper names (of places and people) and in words borrowed from foreign languages. Unlike English, all letters in Estonian are pronounced (for example: the silent k in "knee").

Letter sounds

a = as in cut
b = similar to "p" in English
g = similar to "k" in English
j = as in yes
r = like in English, but rolled
š = "sh"
ž = as in pleasure
õ = as in own
ä = as in bat
ö = similar to the "u" in fur
ü = as in cube

Letter combinations

Some combined letters in Estonian have special pronunciations.

ai = as in aisle
ei = as in vein
oo = as in water
uu = as in boot
öö = as in fur

Some useful points to remember:
Usually the first syllable of a word is stressed. However, quite a few words with foreign origins and some native Estonian words, such as aitäh, don't follow this pattern.
Vowels and consonants can be short (written with one letter), long or extra long (written with two letters).

In an Emergency

Help!	**Appi!**	awpy
Stop!	**Peatuge!**	beh-atu-gay
Call a doctor.	**Kutsuge arst**	coot-soo-gay arst
Call an ambulance.	**Kutsuge kiirabi**	coot-soo-gay keer-awbi
Call the police.	**Kutsuge politsei**	coot-soo-gay po-leet-say
Call the fire department.	**Kutsuge tuletõrje**	coot-soo-gay too-lei-tur-ye
Where is the nearest telephone?	**Kus on lähim telefon?**	coos onn la-him telefon?
Where is the nearest hospital?	**Kus on lähim haigla?**	coos onn la-him high-glaa?

Communication Essentials

Yes/No	**Jah/Ei**	yah/ey
Please	**Palun**	pa-loon
Thank you	**Aitäh**	ai-tah
Excuse me	**Vabandage**	va-ban-da-gay
Hello	**Tere**	te-re
Goodbye	**Head aega**	heyad ayga
Good night	**Head õhtut**	heyad ewh-toot
morning	**hommik**	hom-mik
afternoon	**pärastlõuna**	pa-rawst-lew-na
evening	**õhtu**	ewh-tu
yesterday	**eile**	eilay
today	**täna**	ta-naw
tomorrow	**homme**	hom-may
What?	**Mida?**	meeda?
When?	**Millal?**	meelal?
Why?	**Miks?**	meeks?
Where?	**Kus?**	coos?

Useful Phrases

How are you?	**Kuidas läheb?**	cooi-das-la-heb?
Very well, thank you.	**Aitäh, väga hästi.**	ai-tah, va-ga has-ti
Pleased to meet you.	**Meeldiv tuttavaks saada.**	mayl-div too-taw-vawks saa-daw
See you soon!	**Varsti näeme!**	vaarsti nay-me!
Where can I get...?	**Kust ma saaksin ...?**	coost ma sawk-sin ...?

How do you get to ...?	**Kuidas minna ...?**	cooi-dass min-na..?
How far is ...?	**Kui kaugel on ...?**	cooi cow-kel onn ...?
Do you speak English?	**Kas te räägite inglise keelt?**	cos tay ra-gi-tay ing-li-say keylt?
I can't speak Estonian.	**Ma ei oska eesti keelt.**	maw ey oska eysti kaylt.
I don't understand.	**Ma ei saa aru.**	Maw ey saw aru
Can you help me?	**Kas saate mind aidata?**	cos-saw-tay meend eye-data?
Please speak slowly.	**Palun rääkige aeglaselt.**	pa-loon ra-ki-gay ayg-la-selt.
Sorry.	**Vabandust.**	va-ban-doost

Making a Telephone Call

Can I call abroad from here?	**Kas ma saan siit välismaale helistada?**	Cos-maw sawn seet va-lees-maw-lay hay-lees-taw-da?
I would like to call collect.	**Tahaksin helistada vastaja kulul.**	Taw-haw-ksin hay-lees-taw-da-vaws-taya-koo-lool.
local call	**kohalik kõne**	kohaw-lik kew-ne
I'll ring back later.	**Helistan hiljem tagasi.**	Hay-lees-tawn heel-yem taw-gaw-si.
Could I leave a message?	**Kas ma saaksin teate jätta?**	Cos maw sawk-seen tyate ya-taw?
Could you speak up a little, please?	**Kas saate natuke valjemini rääkida?**	Cos saw-tay naw-too-kay vawl-ye-meenee ra-ki-daw?

Useful Words

big	**suur**	suur
small	**väike**	vayke
hot	**kuum**	coom
cold	**külm**	kewlm
good	**hea**	he-ya
bad	**halb**	halb
enough	**küllalt**	cool-alt
well	**hästi**	hasti
open	**avatud**	aw-va-tud
closed	**suletud**	soo-laytud
left	**vasak**	vaw-sawk
right	**parem**	paw-rem
straight	**otse**	ot-say
near	**lähedal**	la-hay-dawl
far	**kaugel**	kaw-ghell
up	**ülal**	oolal
down	**all**	all
early	**vara**	va-raw
late	**hilja**	hill-yaw
entrance	**sissepääs**	see-say-pa-es
exit	**väljapääs**	val-yaw-pa-es
toilet	**tualett**	too-a-lett
free/unoccupied	**vaba**	vaw-baw
free/no charge	**tasuta**	taw-soo-taw

Shopping

How much is this?	**Kui palju see maksab?**	Cooi pawl-yu say mawk-sab?
I would like ...	**Tahaksin ...**	taw-hawk-sin ..
Do you have ...?	**Kas teil on ...?**	cos tayl onn ..?
I'm just looking.	**Vaatan lihtsalt.**	vaw-tan liht-sawlt
Do you take credit cards?	**Kas krediit-kaardiga saab maksta?**	cos kre-diit-kawrd-eega sawb mawk-sta?
What time do you open/close?	**Mis kell teil avatakse/suletakse?**	Mees kell tayl a-vaw-tawk-say/su-lay-tawk-say?
this one	**see**	cee
that one	**too**	toe
expensive	**kallis**	kaw-lees
cheap	**odav**	oh-dav
size	**suurus**	soo-rus
antique dealer	**antiigipood**	an-tiiki-pode
souvenir shop	**suveniiripood**	sou-ve-niiri-pode
bookshop	**raamatupood**	raw-maw-too-pode
café	**kohvik**	koh-fik
chemist	**apteek**	ap-tayk
newspaper kiosk	**ajalehekiosk**	a-ya-le-he-kii-osk
department store	**kaubamaja**	cow-ba-mawya
market	**turg**	toorg

Sightseeing

bus	**buss**	boos
tram	**tramm**	trawm
trolley bus	**troll**	trol
train	**rong**	row-ng
bus stop	**bussipeatus**	boo-si-peya-toos

tram stop	**trammipeatus**	tra-mi-peya-toos
art gallery	**kunstigalerii**	koonsti-gale-ree
palace	**palee**	pa-lay
castle	**loss**	lowss
cathedral	**katedraal**	caw-tay-dral
church	**kirik**	kee-reek
garden	**aed**	eye-ed
library	**raamatukogu**	raw-maw-too-kogu
museum	**muuseum**	mu-seum
tourist information	**turismiinfo**	too-ris-me-info
closed for public holiday	**külastajatele suletud puhkepäev**	koo-las-taya-tayle soo-le-tood pooh-ke-payev
travel agent	**reisibüroo**	ray-see-bu-roh

Staying in a Hotel

Have you any vacancies?	**Kas teil on vaba tuba?**	cos tayl onn vawba too ba
double room with double bed	**kahene tuba laia voodiga**	ka-hay-ne tooba la-ya vo-diga
twin room	**kahe voodiga tuba**	ka-hay vo-diga tooba
single room	**ühene tuba**	ew-hene tooba
non smoking	**mittesuitse-tajatele**	meetay-sooitse-ta-ya-lay
room with a bath/shower	**tuba vanniga/ dušiga**	too-ba vaw-niga/ doosh-iga
porter	**portjee**	port-ye
key	**võti**	vew-ti
I have a reservation.	**Mul on reserveeritud.**	Mool onn re-se-veri-tood

Eating Out

A table for ... please	**Palun üks laud ... inimesele**	pa-loon ooks la-ood ... eenee-me-selay
I want to reserve a table.	**Tahaksin reser-veerida lauda**	taw-hawk-sin re-ser-veri-da la-ooda
The bill, please	**Palun arve**	pa-loon arvay
I am a vegetarian.	**Olen taimetoitlane**	Olayn tai-may-toyt-lanay
I'd like ...	**Tahaksin ...**	ta-hawk-sin ...
waiter/ waitress	**kelner/ ettekandja**	kel-ner/ etay-kandya
menu	**menüü**	men-oo
wine list	**veinimenüü**	veini-men-oo
chef's special	**firmaroog**	feer-ma-rogue
tip	**jootraha**	yot-rawha
glass	**klaas**	klas
bottle	**pudel**	poo-del
knife	**nuga**	noo-ga
fork	**kahvel**	kawf-fel
spoon	**lusikas**	loo-si-kaws
breakfast	**hommikusöök**	hom-miku-sook
lunch	**lõuna**	lewna
dinner	**õhtusöök**	euh-tu-sook
main courses	**praed**	prayed
starters	**eelroad**	el-rowad
vegetables	**köögiviljad**	koo-gi-vilyad
desserts	**magustoidud**	maw-gus-toy-dud
rare	**pooltoores**	pole-toe-res
well done	**küps**	cewps

Menu Decoder

äädikas	a-di-kaws	vinegar
aurutatud	ow-ru-tawtud	steamed
friikartul	free-kartool	chips
grillitud	grilly-tud	grilled
jäätis	ya-tis	ice cream
juust	youst	cheese
kala	kaw-la	fish
kana	kawna	chicken
kartul	kar-tool	potatoes
kaste	kaws-tey	sauce
keedetud	kay-day-tud	boiled
klimbid	klim-bid	dumplings
kohv	k-oh-v	coffee
kook, saiad	coke, sigh-ad	cake, pastry
koor	core	cream
küüslauk	koos-lauk	garlic
lambaliha	lawm-ba-leeha	lamb
leib/sai	layb/sei	bread
liha	lee-ha	meat
loomaliha	lo-ma-leeha	beef
mereannid	mayrey-awnid	seafood
mineraalvesi	min-e-rawl-vaysi	mineral water
muna	moona	egg
õli	ewli	oil
õlu	ewlu	beer
pannkook	pawn-coke	pancake
peekon	paykon	bacon
piim	peem	milk
pipar	peepar	pepper
pirukas	piru-kaws	pie